THE AUDACITY OF DECEIT

THE AUDACITY OF DECEIT

BARACK OBAMA'S WAR ON AMERICAN VALUES

BRAD O'LEARY

WND BOOKS

THE AUDACITY OF DECEIT: Barack Obama's War on American Values

A WND Books Book
Published by WND Books, Inc.
Los Angeles, CA

Cover Design by Linda Daly

WND Books books are distributed to the trade by:

Midpoint Trade Books
27 West 20th Street, Suite 1102
New York, NY 10011

WND Books books are available at special discounts for bulk purchases. WND Books also publishes books in electronic formats. For more information call (310) 961-4170 or visit www.wndbooks.com.

First Edition

ISBN: 10-Digit 1935071025
ISBN: 13-Digit 9781935071020
E-Book ISBN: 10-Digit 1935071564
E-Book ISBN: 13-Digit 9781935071563

Library of Congress Control Number: 2008932744

Printed in the United States of America

10 9 8 7 6 5 4 3 2 1

To my six daughters and my voting-age grandchildren. I wrote this book to provide them with enough information to make a clear choice.

TABLE OF CONTENTS

Preface

PREFACE

T*HE AUDACITY OF DECEIT* is a book about Barack Obama, the candidate for president whose soaring rhetoric promises "change." His policies, however, could destroy America as we know it.

President Jimmy Carter's rock-bottom economy of double-digit inflation and unemployment gave way to Ronald Reagan's program of tax and spending cuts that brought about an economic revival that's lasted nearly thirty years. That growth, coupled with technological innovation (computers, Internet, cell phones, and more), lifted millions out of poverty and created America's greatest sustained wave of prosperity ever. The success of Reaganomics speaks for itself: By the time President Reagan left office, the stock market had tripled in value and it then tripled itself again over the next ten years; American wealth had increased by $15 trillion; every income quintile during the Reagan years gained income; and, by 1989, there were 6 million more Americans whose salaries exceeded $50,000 a year, while the number of Americans earning less than $10,000 fell by 3.4 million workers.

Is this the economic success that Obama promises, or is he a Jimmy Carter protégé who wants us all to think that the success of the last thirty years has been wrong and that the only way to rectify this injustice is to redistribute those "ill-gotten" gains?

Obama is hustling America into thinking he is "change," but then again, Herbert Hoover promised change, too.

Can we have universal healthcare without reduced care and long lines? Will America join in the policies of the United Nations, or will she remain a sovereign leader in foreign policy? Do we pay too much in taxes, or too little? Will our free trade policies lead to greater economic success, or cost the U.S. more jobs and raise unemployment?

Will felons be able to vote in future elections? Where does the Second Amendment stand in Barack Obama's eyes, and how will the U.S. Supreme Court be reshaped by an Obama presidency? Will an energy policy predicated upon alternative-fuel development lead to energy independence under President Obama? Does Obama's childhood abandonment affect his policies and judgments?

The Audacity of Deceit examines the Obama record and his proposals on the issues that promise to be at the forefront in this year's pivotal presidential election.

Obama's soaring evangelical rhetoric lulls unwary, unquestioning voters. Obama holds sway with utopian notions that his proposed administration of unity, bipartisanship, and compromise will bring about "change." He tells us that those who disagree with his policies can be bent and guided so that dissent will be a thing of the past. But Obama's Smooth Talk Express is a triumph of style over substance.

America was founded by immigrants from many parts of the world who tolerated the beliefs of others and fought against government tyranny in their lives. In the process, our forefathers created a republic of diverse citizens and lawmakers that found ways to solve our country's problems without morphing into one-party rule.

Should Obama win, however, he'll likely have a veto-proof Congress, as Republicans will likely lose four to seven U.S. Senate seats and as many as thirty House seats, giving his administration dictatorial one-party power. Further, he would have the power to appoint activist judges to the U.S. Supreme Court who could tip the balance of the court and its direction.

President Barack Obama, controlled by the far Left wing of the Democratic party, with a veto-proof Congress and an activist judiciary, could reduce the value of the dollar, lose control of inflation, reduce our exports, strip us of our Second Amendment rights, legalize late-term abortions on demand, and implement tax and regulatory policies that would strangle our economy.

Will you allow Obama's soaring rhetoric to turn off your mind, stifle your dissent, and cause you to accept extreme, misguided remedies to our nation's challenges?

The next president will determine the destiny of our country. That president should be a man whose character and values are yours, so listen carefully.

Special thanks to Jon Dougherty, Tim McGinnis, Peyton Knight, Thuy Ngo, Ann Weems, Bill Parkerson, and Aaron Klein. And a special acknowledgement to a friend of mine, who suggested this book be written.

CHAPTER ONE

CHANGING AMERICA'S SOCIAL VALUES

"I think he [Obama] is deliberately distorting the traditional understanding of the Bible to fit his own worldview, his own confused theology."[1]

—Dr. James Dobson

THE NEXT PRESIDENT of the United States will exert a significant and lasting influence over the moral and spiritual direction of our Judeo-Christian nation. Whether it's federal policy on taxpayer-funded abortion and embryonic stem cell research, or parental notification for minors seeking abortion, or the restoration of the marriage tax penalty, the next president will champion policies that support the family or tear it down; respect the sanctity of life or devalue it; defend the institution of marriage or erode the social glue that holds our nation together.

The vast majority of the American middle class identifies with the Judeo-Christian belief system. But Senator Barack Obama seems to challenge these voters' religious values and moral beliefs. He seems firmly ensconced in the "everything is relative" school of thought that muddles clear definitions or convictions about right and wrong. President Obama would likely impose a gray scale of morality.

Obama's own moral traditions emerge from twenty-seven years of upbringing by an atheist mother, a morally challenged bigamist Muslim-turned-atheist father, and a Muslim stepfather.

From ages six through ten, Obama attended Muslim and Indonesian schools and was exposed to the leadership style of Muslim dictator Suharto, who reigned over Indonesia during Obama's time there. Obama was later influenced by a twenty-year relationship with the Trinity United Church of Christ and its doctrine of Christian Black Liberation Theology—a substitute for the Judeo-Christian belief system that uses the Sunday pulpit to preach victimization and promote wealth redistribution. According to Chicago politician Toni Preckwinkle, her friend Obama joined Trinity after she suggested that it would provide him with "lots of social connections and prominent parishioners" and is "a good place for a politician to be a member."[2]

Obama's long membership in Trinity has instilled in the would-be president a firm faith not just in multiculturalism, but also in ethical relativism and the supremacy of *feelings*. As best-selling author and religious ethicist Dennis Prager puts it:

> The Left's opposition to Judeo-Christian values is first and foremost an opposition to objective, or universal, ethics. Ethics and morality are relative. There is no objective or universal standard of right and wrong. We are each the source of our own values.[3]

At a San Francisco fundraising event just before the 2008 Pennsylvania and Indiana presidential primaries, Obama was asked what he thought about the middle-class, blue-collar voters he was trying to attract to his candidacy. In what he apparently thought was an off-the-record remark, Obama said:

> [I]t's not surprising…that they [voters] get bitter, they cling to guns or religion or antipathy to people who aren't like them or anti-immigrant sentiment or anti-trade sentiment as a way to explain their frustrations."[4]

Clinging to religion? Is that what people of faith are doing when they support the difference between right and wrong, when they express their belief in God? Clearly, we must question Barack Obama's claim to share the fundamental values of Judeo-

Christian, working-class church-going Americans. Therefore, an essential question for voters is this: Does Obama believe that the moral values of an atheist—or a Muslim, Hindu, Buddhist, or Christian Black Liberation theologian—should have equal value in public policy to the moral beliefs of Judeo-Christians? It seems so.

A Harvard-educated elitist, Obama will likely staff his administration with like-minded activists bent on promoting policies that would corrode the moral ties that have historically bound us together as a nation.

As nationally syndicated columnist Cal Thomas observes:

> Obama is better at biblical language and imagery than any Democrat in modern times...
>
> "I'm rooted in the Christian tradition," said Obama. He then adds something most Christians will see as universalism: "I believe there are many paths to the same place, and that is a belief that there is a higher power, a belief that we are connected as a people."...[5]
>
> Evangelicals and serious Catholics might ask if this is so, why did Jesus waste His time coming to Earth, suffering pain, rejection, and crucifixion? If there are many ways to God, He might have sent down a spiritual version of table manners and avoided the rest...
>
> Obama can call himself anything he likes, but there is a clear requirement for one to qualify as a Christian and Obama doesn't meet that requirement. One cannot deny central tenets of the Christian faith, including the deity and uniqueness of Christ as the sole mediator between God and man, and be a Christian. Such people do have a label applied to them in Scripture. They are called "false prophets."[6]

The problem, as Christian minister and broadcaster David R. Stokes points out, is that many will likely be fooled by Obama's religious deception:

> [Q]uoting stuff out of context is commonplace among politicians and spindoctors.

> Why is this kind of thing effective with people who should know better—those who profess to believe the Bible and follow Jesus? Well, the sad fact is that we are dealing with an often underestimated and ignorant illiteracy in many evangelical circles today. As more and more people find theology and doctrine dry and irrelevant, and matters of the soul, eternal life, and moral imperatives not nearly as important as SOCIAL ACTION, the situation is ripe to be exploited by someone with a message that sounds right.

> St. Paul put it this way in some of his last written words: "For the time will come when men will not put up with sound doctrine. Instead, to suit their own desires, they will gather around them a great number of teachers to say what their itching ears want to hear."I Timothy 4:3 (New International Version)[7]

In reality, "compassion" in Barack Obama's hands will mean that big government—not individuals, churches, or private charities—will provide care services, from the cradle to the grave.

CHRISTIAN BLACK LIBERATION THEOLOGY

Barack Obama's campaign regularly touted his twenty-year membership in Chicago's Trinity United Church of Christ as proof of his devotion to Christianity *until* Obama announced his decision to leave his church in May 2008. But a closer look at Obama's longtime church reveals that Trinity practices—and preaches—a different kind of Christianity than most American Christians find at their churches.

National Review Online contributor Stanley Kurtz reviewed two years of *Trumpet Newsmagazine*, a monthly glossy publication founded by Obama's notorious spiritual mentor, Reverend Jeremiah Wright. Kurtz concluded that Wright, who serves as *Trumpet*'s CEO, practiced a Black Liberation Theology brand of Christianity, seeing "his own form of Christianity as profoundly different from Christianity as typically practiced by most American whites and blacks."[8]

This raises new questions about Obama's Christian views and his own "Black Liberation Theology." Featured on *Trumpet*'s cover several times, Obama also granted an exclusive, lengthy interview to the magazine in 2007.

Kurtz reported that, in many issues of *Trumpet*, Wright demonstrated that he emulates the ideology of James Cone, considered the founder of Black Liberation Theology. Cone's main thesis is that true Christianity is specific to the black liberation experience, while traditional Christianity, as commonly practiced in the U.S., is racist and not "true" Christianity.

Acton Institute scholar Anthony B. Bradley provides insight into Cone and his Black Liberation Theology:

> James Cone, the chief architect of Black Liberation Theology in his book *A Black Theology of Liberation* (1970), develops black theology as a system. In this new formulation, Christian theology is a theology of liberation—a rational study of the being of God in the world in light of the existential situation of an oppressed community, relating the forces of liberation to the essence of the gospel, which is Jesus Christ," writes Cone. Black consciousness and the black experience of oppression orient black liberation theology—i.e., one of victimization from white oppression.
>
> For Cone, no theology is Christian theology unless it arises from oppressed communities and interprets Jesus' work as that of liberation. In Cone's context, the great event of Christ's liberation was freeing African Americans from the centuries-old tyranny of white racism and white oppression....
>
> One of the pillars of Obama's home church, Trinity United Church of Christ, is "economic parity." On the Web site, Trinity claims that God is not pleased with "America's economic mal-distribution."...
>
> Black Liberation theologians James Cone and Cornel West have worked diligently to embed Marxist thought into the black church since the 1970s. For Cone, Marxism best addressed remedies to the condition of blacks as victims of white oppression. In *For My People*, Cone explains that "the Christian faith does not possess in its nature the means for analyzing the

structure of capitalism. Marxism as a tool of social analysis can disclose the gap between appearance and reality, and thereby help Christians to see how things really are."[9]

Thus, Cone's brand of Christianity strongly denounces any Christian practice that doesn't espouse this specific political approach—one that is redistributionist and liberation-focused. And Chicago's Trinity United Church of Christ, Reverend Wright, and his *Trumpet Newsmagazine* consistently express views consistent with Cone's tradition of Christianity.

Attacking conservative Christians as "emulating those who killed Jesus, rather than following the practice of Jesus himself," Black Liberation theologian Obery M. Hendricks, Jr. contributed an article to the April 2007 issue of *Trumpet*. "Many good church-going folk have been deluded into behaving like modern-day Pharisees and Sadducees when they think they're really being good Christians," contended Hendricks. "George Bush and his unwitting prophets of Baal," he wrote, "may well prove to be the foremost distorters of the true practice of Jesus' Gospel of peace, liberation, and love ever seen in modern times."[10]

In an August 2007 issue of *Trumpet*, Wright argued that Jesus is "African," and he attacks "white" Christianity as make-believe. "How do I tell my children," Wright wrote, "about the African Jesus who is not the guy they see in the picture of the blond-haired, blue-eyed guy in their Bible or the figment of white supremacists [sic] imagination that they see in Mel Gibson's movies?" Authentic, liberation Christianity, pens Wright, "is far more than the litmus test given by some Gospel music singers and much more than the cosmetic facade of make-pretend white Christianity." What's more, Wright denounces "colored preachers" who don't subscribe to Black Liberation Theology as people who "hate themselves, who hate black people, who desperately want to be white and who write and say stupid things in public to make 'Masa' feel safer."

In his analysis of *Trumpet*, Kurtz found that Wright embraces white preachers who toe Cone's line of Black

Liberation Theology. The now infamous Chicago Catholic pastor Michael Pfleger, whom Obama himself identified as a close associate and spiritual guide, is such a proselyte. "Faith is key to his life, no question about it," Pfleger told the *Chicago Sun-Times* of Obama in 2004. "It is central to who he is, and not just in his work in the political field, but as a man, as a black man, as a husband, as a father.... I don't think he could easily divorce his faith from who he is."[11] But Obama did try for a quick, politically expedient divorce from his church, denouncing Pfleger himself during the 2008 presidential primary after the pastor accused Senator Hillary Clinton of being a white supremacist who probably thought she was entitled to the White House because of her skin color.[12]

Kurtz argues it is "inconceivable" that Obama, featured on the cover and inside many editions of *Trumpet*, was not aware of the magazine and its content. According to Kurtz, the magazine features Wright's radical views "everywhere—in the pictures, the headlines, the highlighted quotations and above all in the articles themselves."[13]

While Obama has spoken generally in interviews about his Christianity, he has not addressed the topic of Black Liberation Theology, perhaps because this doctrine and its Marxist tinge run contrary to the Judeo-Christian values that the American voting majority holds dear. As medical doctor and columnist Ronald Cherry reminds us:

> In Judeo-Christian America, one finds the idea of equality before God and the law, but not government-forced economic equality. Modern European culture has stressed the value of economic equality rather than Liberty, and their governments unjustly enforce the principle. This has led to the failed European inventions of Socialism and Communism. Socialists in America have been lured into this failed European idea of social justice.
>
> Socialism is a failure in that it unjustly suppresses human creativity by excessively taxing away its rewards, and by foolishly giving economic reward to many who, even though mentally and physically able, fail to honor their Divine privilege

and duty to work creatively. Thus, Socialism is a dual insult to God-given creativity. Communism was much worse in that it also dishonored the sacredness of human life and liberty. Communism was the inevitable result of separating not just church from state, but separating God from state. Communism dishonored God's gifts of Life, Liberty, and Creativity.[14]

America is a Christian nation founded on Judeo-Christian values. But Barack Obama has supported another concept. In fact, in at least two comments that few reporters noticed, Obama declared that the U.S. is "no longer a Christian nation," but also a nation of others, including Muslims and nonbelievers.

"Whatever we once were," Obama said during a June 2007 speech, "we're no longer a Christian nation. At least not just. We are also a Jewish nation, a Muslim nation, and a Buddhist nation, and a Hindu nation, and a nation of nonbelievers."[15]

Asked to clarify his remarks, Obama simply repeated them. "I think that the right might worry a bit more about the dangers of sectarianism," he wrote in an email to Christian Broadcast Network senior correspondent David Brody. "Whatever we once were, we're no longer just a Christian nation; we are also a Jewish nation, a Muslim nation, a Buddhist nation, a Hindu nation, and a nation of nonbelievers."[16]

OBAMA AND THE NATION OF ISLAM

While the media has gone to great lengths to portray Obama as a friend of Christians and Christian leaders, Obama's personal associations paint a different picture. For example, when interviewed for this book, Malik Zulu Shabazz recently said, "Of course there are connections between Obama's associates and the Nation of Islam." Shabazz is the national chairman of the New Black Panther Party (NBPP), whose official platform:

- states "white man has kept us deaf, dumb and blind";

- refers to the "white racist government of America";

- demands black people be exempt from military service;

- and uses the word "Jew" repeatedly in quotation marks.[17]

Shabazz was also in the audience for Reverend Wright's highly publicized National Press Club speech in Washington, D.C. in April 2008, when Obama's then-pastor defended Nation of Islam head Louis Farrakhan as "one of the most important voices in the 20th and 21st century."[18]

While Obama strongly condemned Wright's remarks and Farrakhan himself, Obama, in fact, enjoyed a close relationship with Wright and his church, which openly lauded Farrakhan and the Nation of Islam—at least until Wright's speech landed Obama in hot water. Before these relationships came to light, Obama, for example, shared the cover of Wright's *Trumpet* magazine with Farrakhan, whom the magazine notoriously bestowed with Wright's *Empowerment Award* in 2007. Obama was also featured on a *Trumpet* cover in an issue entitled, "The Legacy Lives On." The cover montage boasts black leadership faces including Obama with Wright, Farrakhan, Nation of Islam founder Elijah Muhammad, and even Johnny Cochran (O.J. Simpson's attorney). Martin Luther King, Jr. was noticeably absent.

In addition, Obama's chief political strategist, David Axelrod, sits on the finance committee of St. Sabina, the Chicago Catholic parish led by none other than Obama's former mentor, Father Pfleger. Pfleger hosted Farrakhan at his parish as late as last May 2008, in Farrakhan's first public appearance since he announced in 2006 he was seriously ill as a result of prostate cancer. According to reports, Pfleger spent hours with the Nation of Islam leader during his illness, and previously enlisted Farrakhan's support for several of his initiatives, including an anti-gun protest in 2007.

Pledged Obama superdelegate Reverend Willie Barrow is a member of the Obama campaign's official Faith Outreach Team. He is also a close friend of Farrakhan's and a staunch supporter of the Nation of Islam. In fact, in a 1999 interview, Farrakhan stated that he met with Barrow to devise his Nation of Islam platforms.[19]

Even more troubling, Obama employed senior staffers who belong to the Nation of Islam, according to *WorldNetDaily* journalist Aaron Klein. A former insider who spoke to Klein on the condition of anonymity expressed particular concern that Obama employed at least two Nation members in his early days as a state senator, when he had only a small budget with which to staff his office. "It is ironic that two of Obama's employees in those days were known Nation of Islam activists," the former insider told Klein, "when Obama employed perhaps a total of maybe three or four staffers."[20] This same insider also confirmed to Klein that Obama was directly aware of the Nation of Islam members on his staff.

ATHEISM AND THE VALUE OF LIFE

As an Illinois state senator, what value system helped to inform Barack Obama's decisions? Were his ethical deliberations founded on a Judeo-Christian moral heritage? Or did he bring Reverend Wright's Christian Black Liberation theology to his job of representing his constituents? Then again, how might a philosophy of atheism come into play for the legislator?

To determine his stand on a wide variety of life issues, the Family Research Council's *Values Voter Guide for 2008 Presidential Candidates* examined Obama's writings, public statements, and voting record. According to the Council's research, Obama supports federal funding of therapeutic cloning research on leftover embryos derived from *in vitro* fertilization and research that would destroy embryonic human life. In fact, Obama would oppose a "federal law prohibiting states from engaging in research in which (or which relies on research in which) a human embryo is destroyed." The report further indicates that Obama would oppose a continuation of President Bush's ban on the use of federal funds for research on human embryonic stem cell lines created after August 2001. And, as president of the United States, he would issue an executive order to lift the embargo on abortions performed on U.S. military bases worldwide.

Asked if he believes that life begins at conception, Obama equivocates and evades. However, when that question is put to Americans, the answer is clear. According to a Fox News/Opinion Dynamics poll, an overwhelming majority of voters believes life begins at conception:[21]

> "Do you believe that human life begins at conception, or once the baby may be able to survive outside the mother's womb with medical assistance, or when the baby is actually born?"
>
> At conception: 55 percent
>
> Survive outside womb: 23 percent
>
> At birth: 13 percent
>
> Not sure: 9 percent

In his 2006 book, *The Audacity of Hope,* Obama says he sides with Supreme Court justices like Stephen Breyer, who voted with the minority in favor of allowing late-term abortions. "I have to side with Justice Breyer's view of the Constitution," Obama wrote, "that it is not a static, but rather a living document and must be read in the context of an ever-changing world."[22] In other words, the United States Constitution is a "living document" that Obama would like to twist and change in order to destroy human life.

Author, columnist, and college professor Mike Adams, a former atheist, provides insight into his own period of godlessness. Interestingly, Adams' former atheistic views on how and why government should function are nearly identical to what Obama currently espouses. "During that dark time of my life I gave nothing to charity. I did no volunteer work. Instead, I railed against the political establishment and demanded radical changes that would move the country drastically further to the left," Adams explains. "I demanded radical leftist tax and welfare schemes that I knew would never be accepted by a majority of the American people. But by making those arguments, I was able to deceive myself into thinking I was a superior moral being."[23]

Adams writes in great detail about present atheist philosophers such as Peter Singer. It is Singer's philosophy that Barack Obama, as a state senator from Illinois, defended.

"Characteristics like rationality, autonomy, and self-consciousness…make a difference," according to Singer. "Infants lack these characteristics. Killing them, therefore, cannot be equated with killing normal human beings, or any other self-conscious beings."[24]

Thus, Singer and other atheists argue that a given human being is worth less than another and it is therefore perfectly acceptable, for example, to allow a viable baby who survived an abortion to lie on a shelf and suffer, sometimes for as long as eight hours, before dying. These atheists—*and* Barack Obama—do not want such a dying child to receive emergency medical care, lest he or she survive.

Although he has only served in the United States Senate since 2005, Barack Obama's record clearly shows that he is not in accord with the majority of Americans when it comes to protecting innocent human life. While most Americans oppose abortion on demand, Obama supports it. While most Americans support parental notification laws, Obama does not. While most Americans want to outlaw gruesome partial birth abortions that kill a partially born, viable baby, Obama does not. Though most Americans want to withhold public financing for abortion, Obama does not. In terms of legislation, his position is clear.

The National Abortion Rights Action League (NARAL), the leading advocate for abortion and partial birth abortion in America today, praised Senator Obama on its Web site for casting "thirteen votes on abortion and other reproductive rights issues." According to NARAL, "All thirteen of those votes were pro-(abortion)."[25]

But a Zogby International poll in July 2008 found that 76 percent of Americans, and 74 percent of women, believe that "a physician should be legally required to notify the parents of an underage girl who requests an abortion." Here, as in all facets of the abortion debate, Obama walks in lockstep with pro-abortion supporters—a slim minority.

According to an ABC News poll, Obama's stance is decidedly outside the mainstream. The fact is that 69 percent of Americans strongly oppose partial birth abortion. And 47 percent oppose abortion in all cases except to save the life of the mother (a view confirmed by the United States Supreme Court in 2007 when it upheld a congressional restriction on the partial birth abortion procedure to "promote respect for life, including the life of the unborn.")[26]

The Supreme Court's 5-4 decision upholding the Partial Birth Abortion Ban Act passed by Congress in 2003 marked the first time justices have agreed that a specific abortion procedure could be banned—a decision with which President Obama would most likely be displeased. Obama has made it clear that, if elected, he will appoint Supreme Court justices who would reverse this ruling.

The partial birth abortion procedure, known as "dilation and extraction," is incredibly barbaric. The process takes two to three days, during which the cervix is gradually forced to dilate. Once the cervix is fully dilated, the doctor uses forceps to grasp the full-term baby and pull him or her out, feet first. The baby is birthed, except for the head, which remains in the birth canal. The doctor then makes an incision at the base of the baby's skull, inserts a suction device into the incision, and removes the child's brain tissue. The dead child is then removed and disposed of.

Even pro-choice Catholic voters may find Barack Obama's view of "choice" too extreme for them. While these voters may not follow their church's teaching, Pope Benedict XVI nevertheless says, "As far as the Catholic Church is concerned, the principal focus of her interventions in the public arena is the protection and promotion of the dignity of the person, and she is thereby consciously drawing particular attention to principles which are not negotiable. Among these the following emerge clearly today...protection of life in all its stages, from the first moment of conception until natural death."[27] As a result, many Catholic bishops are denying Communion to more and more Catholic politicians who favor "choice" and abortion.

But even by pro-choice standards and even in politics, Obama takes the disrespect for human life to boundaries seldom seen. According to author and columnist Amanda Carpenter, Obama's "radical stance on abortion puts him further left on that issue than even NARAL Pro-Choice America."[28] In fact, during his tenure as a state senator, *Obama fought successfully to keep blatant infanticide legal in Illinois.*

When a newborn has complications or requires complex surgery, doctors and nurses do everything in their power to save the life of the child. However, at Christ Hospital in Illinois, registered nurse Jill Stanek discovered that babies who survived abortions and were born alive were not given care. Instead, these babies were "shelved to die in the soiled utility room"[29] — an agonizing death that sometimes can take up to eight hours.[30]

Stanek spoke up about this horror of horrors, and in 2001, she told the Illinois Senate:

> Christ Hospital unveiled its "Comfort Room." So now I can no longer say that live aborted babies are left in our soiled utility room to die. We now have this prettily wallpapered room complete with a First Foto machine, baptismal gowns, a footprinter and baby bracelets, so that we can offer keepsakes to parents of their aborted babies. There is even a nice wooden rocker in the room to rock live aborted babies to death.[31]

Unmoved, Obama responded to Stanek's testimony. "Ms. Stanek, your initial testimony last year showed your dismay at the lack of regard for human life," Obama said before the Illinois State General Assembly. "I agreed with you last year, and we suggested that there be a Comfort Room or something of that nature be done. The hospital acknowledged that and changes were made and you are still unimpressed. It sounds to me like you are really not interested in how these fetuses are treated, but rather not providing absolutely any medical care or life to them."[32]

Stanek was stunned. "Obama may have thought it impressive to wrap the baby one was killing in a blanket surrounded by silk flowers rather than leave him naked on a steel sink sideboard but he was right—I was nonplussed," she recounted. "I responded: 'What the hospital did was try to make things look better. What it really is, is that the baby is still dead.'" Stanek added that she didn't recognize it at the time, but she was "describing future presidential candidate Barack Obama's campaign: attempting to repackage liberal extremism to look comforting."[33]

In fact, in 2001, Obama was the sole opponent to speak out on the Illinois Senate floor against legislation designed to protect viable, living babies who survive late-term abortions. "I just want to suggest…that this is probably not going to survive constitutional scrutiny," he acknowledged in voting against the legislation. "Number one, whenever we define a pre-viable fetus as a person that is protected by the equal protection clause or the other elements in the Constitution, what we're really saying is, in fact, that they are persons that are entitled to the kinds of protections that would be provided to—a child, a nine-month-old child that was delivered to term."[34]

In 2003, the legislation was referred to the Health and Human Services Committee. Barack Obama chaired the committee and made certain that the bill never came up for a vote.[35]

Former Illinois State Senator Patrick O'Malley served with Obama on the Judiciary Committee. "On the one hand [Obama] holds himself out to be a constitutional scholar, and, of course, our Constitution makes clear that persons born are entitled to all the rights and privileges of full citizens," O'Malley said of Obama's persistence against the bill. "He consistently characterized the issue before us as being about abortion, but the legislation had nothing to do with *Roe v. Wade*. It focused on persons born alive. It was so easy to be on the right side of the angels here, but he wasn't."[36]

Jill Stanek, too, remained perplexed by Obama's ruthless battle to make sure that pre-term babies who survive abortion and are born alive should be left to die. "He was on the wrong side of politics, too," Stanek recounts. "By the third time Obama tried to snuff Born Alive, he was running for the U.S. Senate. The federal version had passed the year before unanimously in the Senate and almost unanimously in the House. Even NARAL went neutral. Pro-aborts agreed to let it pass without a fight lest they appear extreme. Except Obama. He decided to battle alone further left than any other senator—Boxer, Clinton, Kennedy, Kerry, *et al*. Risky. Odd."[37]

Stanek's curiosity led her into an investigation in which she discovered a connection between Obama's church and Christ Hospital. Stanek found that Obama's pastor, Rev. Jeremiah Wright, served on the board of directors of Evangelical Health Systems, which later became Advocate Health Care. Wright's church (Trinity United Church of Christ) jointly controlled and operated Advocate Health Care, and one of Advocate's properties just happens to be Christ Hospital. Trinity Church is also a member of the Religious Coalition for Reproductive Choice, a rabid pro-abortion group.[38]

"Which explanation makes more sense?" asks Stanek. "That the fire rose in Obama's belly to fight for what he nobly, but foolishly, thought was the sacred right to infanticide...Or that Advocate got to Obama through its Trinity United Church of Christ contacts?"[39]

Regardless of whether Obama was carrying water for his pro-abortion pastor and church, or fighting for a personal belief that some babies born alive should be left to die, one thing is clear: *His actions are far outside the mainstream values of most Americans.*

According to a July 2008 Zogby International poll, 68 percent of Americans believe that "a doctor should give medical care to a fetus that survives an abortion." Only 15 percent believe that such care should be withheld. (The remaining 17 percent have no opinion). Moreover, the poll shows that 65 percent of Democrats believe such babies should be given medical care, as do:

- 68 percent of Independents;

- 59 percent of self-described "Liberals";

- 68 percent of women;

- and 56 percent of those who say they *never* attend church.

The Zogby poll further found that 53 percent of all Americans, and 56 percent of women, believe that "abortion destroys a human life and is manslaughter."

As these polling numbers show, the "choice" that most women make is in opposition to abortion.

The product of atheist parents and a Muslim stepfather, Obama understandably would want to convey the impression that Muslim, Hindu, Buddhist, atheist, and humanist views and values are equal and akin to Judeo-Christian beliefs. But they are not. The essential issue, then, is whether these religions and philosophies should be given equal standing in the public policy arena if they do not reflect the beliefs of most Americans. Specifically, how does Obama justify his stance in his battle to deny medical care to viable babies? And can America tolerate a president who may rely on atheistic reasoning in matters of life and death?

MARRIAGE

The more we explore Barack Obama's social positions, the clearer the picture becomes of Obama's America. For example, will he promote traditional marriage and a broad range of policies that will strengthen the family? Or will President Obama adopt policies that discourage marriage, insert government between parent and child, and impose anything-goes, "progressive" values on our society?

Under an Obama administration, we can expect the federal government to attack traditional values and overwhelm the manpower and financial resources of the conservative movement—on a vast variety of fronts. From abolishing the "Don't Ask, Don't Tell" policy on gays in the military to redefining marriage as something other than a union between a man and woman, from banishing expressions of faith in the public square to teaching six-year-old children about sex—including homosexuality—Barack Obama's America will rush headlong into moral chaos, straining the ties that bind us together as a people. Gay marriage will be just one manifestation of this change. Obama will not only force us to accept gay marriage, but will also assert that gay lifestyles are morally equivalent to Christian lifestyles.

On record against a constitutional amendment defining marriage as the legal union of one man and one woman, Obama also opposes the core goals of the 1996 Federal Defense of Marriage Act, a law designed to strengthen the traditional family.[40] Given the chance, Obama would seek to repeal or severely modify the act and nullify its intent in favor of, presumably, alternative family definitions that include same-sex partnerships. Obama has made it clear that he supports the 2008 California Supreme Court decision granting gays the right to civil law marriages. So what changes will come if gays gain the right to marry?

First, all case law governing divorce would have to be changed; those changes will certainly affect custody and case law governing heterosexual marriages. But these are not simple changes. Literally thousands of child custody rulings, state laws, and other legal precedents would be reconsidered and turned upside down.

Once federal and state laws uphold gay marriage, gays will be entitled to sue anyone licensed by the state that refuses to perform a marriage, which would run counter to the beliefs of most Americans. According to a 2008 Zogby International poll, 64 percent of Americans believe that, if gays are permitted to legally marry, they should *not* be permitted to sue religions, churches, or priests who refuse to perform gay marriages. Yet, on the gay marriage issue, Obama's goal is not to end discrimination of gays, but to force all Americans and religions to accept homosexuality as equal in moral value to heterosexuality. No doubt President Obama will face an uphill battle.

OBAMA'S ZERO-TO-FIVE PROGRAM

Incredibly, Obama would like to begin indoctrinating children with his brand of extremism at the earliest stages of development. He plans to implement what he calls a "zero to five" plan, which he says would place a "key emphasis at early care and education for infants."[41] This program would mandate government childcare centers for children up to five years of age. The price tag? $10 billion. None of this money would go to religious institutions, as some Head Start funds do. Rather, "zero to five" programs would likely be devoid of all Judeo-Christian thought and the children enrolled in the program would be taught only secular, government, and "universal" values. Of course, the similarities between this program and those in communist and fascist countries are evident. This is Obama's America.

The plan is perhaps symptomatic of Obama's own childhood, when he was abandoned by his father. But, in terms of policy, it is most likely that Obama intends to replace the Judeo-Christian values that are traditionally taught to young children in the home environment, with his own brand of secular values. How to accomplish this? The only way, of course, is to remove infants and young children from their homes, herding them into government schools where their innocent minds can be infiltrated before parents, churches, or youth groups have a chance to influence them with traditional values.

SUMMARY

Barack Obama demonstrates only contempt for traditional Christian values. Ignoring the fact that our free nation was founded on those values, he seems to believe that Christian voters should not inject their moral values into any policy decision. People who believe in traditional marriage, who pay their taxes, who love our nation, and are trying to raise their families in a God-fearing environment are belittled by Obama and Hollywood (including Obama supporters Rosie O'Donnell, Oliver Stone, and Ben Affleck), smeared by the secular Left and ridiculed by leftist Democrats in Congress. In addition, Obama and his followers:

- Support so-called "diversity training" that compels acceptance of "alternative lifestyles" and the passage of "hate crime" laws that criminalize what people say and do;

- Oppose the Marriage Protection Amendment to the U.S. Constitution;

- Want to impose the gay agenda on society, including acceptance of "civil unions," "domestic partnership" laws, and other special rights for gays;

- Want to install political correctness and speech "codes" at our colleges and universities to punish students who hold traditional values;

- Would like to force sex education in public schools, including kids as young as five and six years of age, and perhaps younger in his zero-to-five program;

- Want taxpayer funding for abortion through Medicare and Medicaid and through our nation's foreign aid spending;

- Approve euthanasia, partial-birth abortion, and other aspects of the death culture;

- Seek to end American foreign aid restrictions on abortions done overseas for gender selection purposes. These abortions, many of which are performed to abort female babies, must never be funded with American tax dollars. In July 2008, a Zogby International poll found that 85 percent of Americans "oppose a woman's right to an abortion based on the sex of the fetus," as do 88 percent of women, 76 percent of Democrats, 80 percent of Independents, 81 percent of self-described "Liberals," and 67 percent of those who say they never attend church.

- Accept vulgar and violent lyrics in popular music that belittle women, demonize police and glorify the street gang culture. Obama himself listens to such songs—with reprehensible lyrics—on his personal iPod. For example, on his iPod, Obama listens to "artist" Jay-Z. In an interview with *Rolling Stone* magazine, Obama praised Jay-Z. "Every time I talk to Jay-Z, who is a brilliant talent and a good guy, I enjoy how he thinks," Obama said. "He's serious and he cares about his art. That's somebody who is going to start branching out and can help shape attitudes in a positive way.[42] Reasonable Americans might be concerned about the work of this man whom

Obama believes "can shape attitudes in a positive way." Here is a taste of his lyrics:

I don't love 'em I f--k 'em.
[...]
She be all on my d--k.
[...]
S--t, I put the rubber on tighter.
[...]*[43]*

In Barack Obama's America, Christians will be told to sit down, shut up, and pay the bills. President Obama will tell Christians that the America in which they grew up is gone, that people of faith have a role to play in public—but only if they leave their moral values at home. With an Obama victory in 2008, Big Brother government, not the people, will be in charge, and Americans will have to accept the anything goes, grayscale morality as the "best thing" for our culture.

The charismatic Obama certainly has a great many supporters in his seductive grip. Some even faint in his presence. Obama paints a gloomy picture of present-day America. He castigates his fellow colleagues on Capitol Hill for being "Washington insiders" (odd, considering that he, himself, is a Washington insider), and promises his disciples hope and change if they follow him—and discard the values they've come to hold dear. Hopefully people will see this fraudulent routine for what it is before it's too late.

As Obama says, he and his supporters can become "a hymn that will heal this nation, repair this world, and make this time different than all the rest." But Obama and his elitist rhetoric is more likely to divide us than unite us.

For new, breaking information on Barack Obama since this book was published, please go to www.audacityofdeceit.com. If you have friends who would like to receive this chapter, or any of the chapters in this book, please refer them to the same Web site where they can download the chapter of their choice for free.

CHAPTER TWO

CHANGING THE SECOND AMENDMENT

"The problem that we've had is that the overwhelming majority of gun owners…would be amenable to reasonable gun control laws.[1]

—Senator Barack Obama

WOULD OBAMA be so understanding if the District of Columbia, New York City, or his own hometown of Chicago—each with ultra-restrictive gun laws—had instead passed a total ban on certain types of free speech, or a law allowing police to conduct any kind of search or seizure they wanted on anyone, at any time and place, without a warrant? Based on what he has said in the past, the answer is a resounding "no." When it comes to other constitutional rights, Obama draws a line. But he is far too willing, even eager, to casually cast aside the people's right to keep and bear arms.

Obama has held his anti-gun and anti-self-defense position since his earliest days in elected office. In 1996, as he was seeking a state senate seat in Illinois, Obama made his disdain for the Second Amendment perfectly clear. When filling out a twelve-page questionnaire for the Independent Voters of Illinois/Independence Precinct Organization (IVI/IPO), he gave detailed answers elaborating on his left-wing views regarding a range of "progressive" (read *liberal*) issues. While he admits his answers to questions about the right to keep and bear arms are correct, they were nonetheless quick, to the point, and decidedly anti-Second Amendment:[2]

> Do you support state legislation to (a) ban the manufacture, sale and possession of handguns? He answered, "Yes."
>
> (b) ban the manufacture, sale and possession of assault weapons? He answered, "Yes."
>
> (c) require mandatory waiting periods, with background checks, to purchase guns? He answered, "Yes."

When tragedy struck Northern Illinois University in Dekalb on Valentine's Day 2008, according to the *Baltimore Sun*, Obama seized that moment to condemn guns and the National Rifle Association. Specifically, Obama referenced a California gun law "that allows micro-tracing of bullets that have been discharged in a crime so that they can immediately be traced."[3] "Ballistic fingerprinting" is a technology that the NRA and law enforcement agencies have repeatedly said not only lends itself to error, but also infringes on the rights of tens of millions of law-abiding Americans.

"[The law] is something that California has passed over the strong objections of the NRA.... That's the kind of common-sense gun law that gun owners as well as victims of gun violence can get behind,"[4] Obama said. Taking advantage of the NIU shootings to plead this case, however, he ignored the fact that, in that case (and most others), the firearm was never in question and a so-called ballistic fingerprint would have been useless and irrelevant. Obama went on to claim allegiance to the Second Amendment, but left the door wide open for added gun regulations. "There is an individual right to bear arms," he claimed, "but it's subject to common sense regulation."[5]

The *Sun* further reported that, "mentioning his home city, Obama said local entities should also have the ability to have their own more strict [gun] regulations."[6] "I think that local jurisdictions have the capacity to institute their own gun laws.... The Cities of Chicago [also San Francisco and New York] have gun laws, as does Washington, D.C.," he said. "I think the notion that somehow local jurisdictions can't initiate gun safety laws to deal with gangbangers and random shootings on the street isn't born [sic] out by our Constitution."[7]

This from a lawyer who claims to be an authority on the U.S. Constitution.

"A-HUNTING WE WILL GO..."

Attempting to portray himself as a pro-gun rights candidate, Barack Obama has turned to a familiar theme: hunting. However, he sponsored an amendment by Senator Ted Kennedy to ban almost all rifle ammunition commonly used for hunting and sport shooting.

"Barack Obama did not hunt or fish as a child," writes Carrie Budoff Brown for the online political journal *Politico.com*. "He lives in a big city. And as an Illinois state legislator and U.S. senator, he consistently backed gun control legislation. But he is nevertheless making a play for pro-gun voters" on the campaign trail.[8]

In an email to the Pennsylvania Federation of Sportsmen's Clubs in late March 2008, the Obama campaign tried to reach out to gun owners, saying Obama would "appreciate all sportsmen taking the time to learn the facts: Our candidate strongly supports the rights and traditions of sportsmen throughout Pennsylvania and the United States of America."[9]

A two-page white paper posted on his campaign Web site assiduously avoids his anti-gun voting record as a legislator. In fact, the site avoids guns and his record of gun control, *period*. Under a heading of "Additional Issues/Sportsmen," the position paper doesn't mention the true intent of the Second Amendment. Instead, it addresses duck hunting and target shooting.[10]

The last sentence belies his true feelings about guns and *our* right to own them. "He also believes," it states, "that the right is subject to *reasonable and commonsense regulation*" (emphasis added). We already know what measures Barack Obama believes constitute "reasonable and commonsense regulation"—outright gun bans, semi-automatic bans, opposition to legally carrying a concealed firearm for protection, closing down gun dealers and stores, and laws allowing only one handgun purchase per month.[11] His rhetoric doesn't reflect his true feelings, but that's an illusion created on purpose, to fool unsuspecting voters.

"THIRD WAY" GUN CONTROL

Obama is seemingly trying to dupe Americans into thinking that he actually supports an individual's right to keep and bear arms. But when we scratch below the surface, we find a radical, anti-gun politician. Period. Like his Democratic rival, Senator Hillary Clinton, Obama uses scripted rhetorical tricks right out of the "progressive" gun prohibitionists' "Third Way" playbook, to the letter. In other words, he is talking *our* talk while walking *their* walk.

Obama's apparent attempt to fool gun rights voters is intentionally opaque, designed for less politically savvy voters.

"The problem that we've had is that the overwhelming majority of gun owners…would be amenable to reasonable gun control laws," Obama said in an April 22, 2007, interview with Radio Iowa. "The NRA's attitude has been that any restriction is an infringement on the rights of gun owners…. I think they are oftentimes able to scare law-abiding gun owners…."[12]

Who's scaring whom? The NRA simply makes voters aware of what Obama really stands for. His record alone is scary enough.

He has embarked on a cynical divide-and-conquer strategy that would lead some firearms owners to believe their Second Amendment rights would be out of harm's way when it comes to his gun control schemes. A recent headline said it all: "Obama: My Wife Sees Need for Rural Gun Ownership."[13] According to the article, Obama argued, "We should be able to combine respect for those traditions with our concern for kids who are being shot down. This is a classic example of us just applying some common sense, just being reasonable, right?"[14]

It does sound "reasonable," doesn't it? That's the point of the "Third Way"—to sound "reasonable" while working toward the ultimate goal of circumventing the Second Amendment.

"Taking Back the Second Amendment" is the "Third Way's" first commandment. As the manifesto advises, "progressives need not change their positions...[but simply] change the rhetoric they employ." So Obama's positions should scream to anyone who has heard his soothing words, "I respect the Second Amendment, *but...*"

That word is always included, and always followed by the inevitable code words, "reasonable" and "common sense," created as cover by the Brady Campaign's gun ban lobbyists.

Try this for "reasonable": As an Illinois candidate for reelection to the state senate, Obama set the "common sense" standard for his gun control stance when he pledged his support for a "1998 National Political Awareness Test" to "ban the sale or transfer of all forms of semi-automatic weapons."[15]

Obama's 1998 position is such a remarkably harsh choice that it has been condemned on even far-left blogs like the *Democratic Underground*. In supporting the goal of banning commerce in "all forms" of semi-automatic weapons, Obama ratcheted up the rhetoric he used in an earlier questionnaire, in which interviewers for the Independent Voters of Illinois garnered his support for a ban on the "manufacture, sale, and possession of handguns."[16]

As an Illinois state senator, Obama was an aggressive advocate for all manner of new gun controls. In a state that has gun owner licensing and *de facto* firearms registration, he pressed for creating mug-shot files and fingerprint databases for law-abiding gun owners. He voted against legislation that would have allowed homeowners to use an affirmative defense when they use firearms to defend themselves and their families against home invaders and burglars—in other words, the right to self-protection.

The true test of his anti-Second Amendment activism, however, is in his service on the ten-member board of directors of the Joyce Foundation, a radical anti-gun money machine.

"The Joyce Foundation is tightly linked to the [billionaire George] Soros Open Society Institute—an extremist group that advocates a worldwide ban on civilian firearm ownership," said one description by an Illinois state gun rights group. "Certainly Barack Obama would not have been invited to sit on the board of the Joyce Foundation had he not held similar views on private firearm ownership."[17]

Doubtless, federal agencies—like the U.S. Department of Justice, the Centers for Disease Control, and the Department of Housing and Urban Development—would use tens of millions of taxpayer dollars to carry out much of this same pervasive, corrosive work, were Obama to ascend to the Oval Office.

PARTIAL RIGHT?

While Obama says the Second Amendment conveys an individual right, every action he takes on the issue says just the opposite. For instance, he firmly maintains that state and local governments retain the right to pass their own gun control agenda, and that such laws are, in turn, constitutional. Just like his stance on the District of Columbia's total handgun ban. Or, say, if you live in a rural area.

"[M]ichelle, my wife, she was traveling up, I think, in eastern Iowa, she was driving through this nice, beautiful area, going through all this farmland and hills and rivers and she said 'Boy, it's really pretty up here,' but she said, 'But you know, I can see why if I was living out here, I'd want a gun,'" Obama said during a campaign stop in western Iowa. "'Because, you know, 9-1-1 is going to take some time before somebody responds. You know what I mean? You know, it's like five miles between every house.'[18]

"So the point is," the candidate continued, "we should be able to do that, and we should be able to enforce laws that keep guns off the streets in inner cities because some unscrupulous gun dealer is, you know, letting somebody load up a van with a bunch of cheap handguns or sawed-off shotguns and dumping them and selling them for a profit in the streets."[19]

Essentially, according to Obama, gun ownership is okay in *some* instances, including hunting, and for protection by those who live in rural areas. But it's *not* okay for others, including Americans who live in much more dangerous settings than Iowa. Like, say, Washington, D.C., where the homicide rate is about a thousand percent higher than it is in eastern Iowa.

Obama's "Third Way" rhetoric is "like saying you have the right to worship as you choose, but the government has the power to ban attending church," writes Kenneth Blackwell, a fellow at the Family Research Council, the American Civil Rights Union, and the Buckeye Institute. "Or that you have the right to free speech, but that government has the power to stop you from speaking about any subject it wants. Or that you have the right against unreasonable searches and seizures, but that anything the government wants to search at your house is automatically reasonable."[20] In fact, our constitutional rights are a government guarantee, not subject to Barack Obama's narrow interpretation.

"REASONABLE" GUN LAWS

What is "reasonable" to a gun banner like Obama is a death knell to our fundamental right to keep and bear arms for the defense of ourselves, our families, and our homes. We know what his idea of "reasonable" is—gun bans, gun registration, gun confiscation.

NRA executive vice president Wayne LaPierre says that, in all the years he has been on the front lines of protecting Second Amendment rights, no conversations have been more sad and more elemental to the future of our freedom than those with activists in a pair of English-speaking nations a world apart.

All of them were good men and women who experienced tyranny and the outright theft of their freedom, their dignity, their honor, and their private property—all made possible by the licensing and registration of their firearms under politicians who said that local governments could enforce reasonable restrictions.

For example, a licensed gun owner in Australia, who first forfeited his registered semi-auto and pump rifles and his self-loading shotguns in 1997, described the gun bans in his country. Holding his most prized possession, a fine Krieghoff Luger, he told LaPierre, "My father fought in World War II. This is the only remembrance of his service that I have. Now I have to give it to the government for destruction."

Asked about resistance, he responded angrily. "If your guns are registered, all of this bravado just withers," he said. "If your firearm is registered you have a choice—you either have to give it up, or you're going to jail. Keep your NRA strong. Don't ever allow the government to register your guns."

Like his Australian counterpart, a licensed gun owner in England had given police obligatory information about his guns, and then was summarily forced to agree to warrantless inspections of his home to check on his gun storage. That was before police took his guns for destruction. He had the same message for Americans: "If they don't know you have firearms, they can't come and take them away from you."

That truth was emphatically repeated by John Crook, who replaced Rebecca Peters as the gun confiscation guru in Australia after she moved to her world gun ban perch with the United Nations. Crook, who headed "Gun Control Australia," said on a *World Today* broadcast interview, "Where there was gun registration, [we] brought in a lot of guns. After all, two-thirds of a million guns is a lot to bring in...."[21]

Those two-thirds of a million *registered* long guns were chopped up and torched, often in front of their duly licensed *former* owners.

Not surprisingly, the Australian ban was followed by an *increase*—not a decrease—in violent crime, which was in turn followed by another round of gun confiscation and destruction, this time of handguns, of which the government did not approve. That war souvenir Luger was among them.

When she pressed for the handgun ban, Peters confessed that her long gun ban was actually aimed at sporting guns and collectibles. "The fact that many civilians owned self-loading or semi-automatic rifles and shotguns for the purpose of sport did not make those guns suitable for civilian ownership—it just meant a lot of unsuitable guns were in circulation," she wrote in November 2002, bragging that her ban "took away nearly 700,000 of them to be melted down into soup cans and bus-stop benches...."[22]

Rather than heed the warnings to preserve our Second Amendment rights, a liberal Congress and Barack Obama—as our next president—will surrender these rights to the likes of Peters and her boss, socialist anti-gun billionnaire George Soros. These are the people who will write the gun ban agenda for the United States. It will begin with "reasonable" requirements, like registration and licensing, and end with turning Americans' guns into soup cans and park benches, and it will continue as the U.S. signs on to a U.N. treaty banning the possession and sale of guns.

Obama will urge the passage of restrictive gun laws in his hometown of Chicago, as well as in cities like New York, Miami, St. Louis, Seattle, Los Angeles, and Washington, D.C., and on every college campus in America, which will leave law-abiding Americans virtually *defenseless* in the face of armed criminals who obviously don't pay attention to gun bans. You can't believe what Obama *says* he means about the Second Amendment. You *can* believe what he's done—and will continue to do—to kill it.

SUPREME COURT UPHOLDS INDIVIDUAL RIGHT

How does Barack Obama propose dealing with the threat of more terrorism on our soil? His primary strategy, besides blaming the current administration for "not doing enough" is to support more gun control while opposing sensible national security measures.

Consider Obama's position, during his presidential campaign, on the U.S. Supreme Court's first Second Amendment case in nearly seven decades. This case may well define the future of an individual's right to keep and bear arms in the United States.

In March 2008, justices heard arguments from District of Columbia lawyers, defending the capital city's total ban on the ownership of handguns, and lawyers for Dick Anthony Heller, a security guard who maintained that the district's ban was a blatant violation of the Constitution. The U.S. District Court of Appeals for the District of Columbia found the law to be unconstitutional.

Where did Obama stand on the case? A month before the appeals court ruled, an interviewer with the online political magazine *Politico.com* quizzed him. "You said recently, 'I have no intention of taking away folks' guns.' But you support the D.C. handgun ban, and you've said that it's constitutional," the reporter pointed out. "How do you reconcile those two positions?"

Obama answered:

> Because I think we have two conflicting traditions in this country. I think it's important for us to recognize that we've got a tradition of handgun ownership and gun ownership generally. And a lot of law-abiding citizens use it [*sic*] for hunting, for sportsmanship, and for protecting their families.

> We also have a violence on the streets that is the result of illegal handgun usage.... We can have a reasonable, thoughtful gun control measures that I think respects the Second Amendment and people's traditions.[23]

Likening the Second Amendment to a "tradition," Obama implies it is merely a custom or ritual, rather than an inalienable right laid out in our Constitution, *the law of the land*.

In early February, fifty-five members of the United States Senate signed a congressional "friend of the court" brief in the *Heller* case, affirming that the Second Amendment protects an individual's right to keep and bear arms (they were joined by the vice president and 250 members of the House of Representatives). Barack Obama refused to sign the brief. Senator John McCain had no problem doing so and was among its first signatories.

In June 2008, the U.S. Supreme Court ruled five to four to uphold the lower court's decision in the *Heller* case—thereby affirming an individual's right to keep and bear arms. Justice Antonin Scalia, who wrote the majority opinion, clearly laid out the precedent for future Second Amendment cases, writing: "[W]whatever else it leaves to future evaluation, it surely elevates above all other interests the right of law-abiding, responsible citizens to use arms in defense of hearth and home."

Yet, as Wayne LaPierre reminds us, the enemies of the Second Amendment are well within striking distance, and an Obama presidency could tip the judicial scales in their favor. LaPierre writes:

> [The majority opinion] was ridiculed by Justice John Paul Stevens as an "overwrought and novel description of the Second Amendment."
>
> Stevens, in his dissent, said the right was solely "to maintain a well-regulated militia." And he said the framers of the Constitution "never evidenced the slightest interest in limiting any legislature's authority to regulate private civilian uses of firearms [as with D.C.'s ban]. Specifically, there is no indication

that the framers of the Amendment intended to enshrine the common-law right of self-defense in the Constitution."

Stevens was joined in dissent by Justices David Souter, Ruth Bader Ginsburg, and Stephen Breyer.

For the majority, Scalia fired back, "[I]t is not the role of this Court to pronounce the Second Amendment extinct."

But consider this. Except for one vote, that is exactly what a Stevens majority would have done.

But for one vote, total bans on firearm ownership would have gotten the *imprimatur* of the high court, and such laws would have metastasized through the efforts of New York billionaire Mayor Mike Bloomberg's *cabal* of big city mayors and his fellow globalist billionaire, George Soros.[24]

Chief Justice Roberts asserted that there is nothing "reasonable" about passing a law in direct contravention of the Constitution—especially a total gun ban. Roberts is right. Note to Obama: The fact is, any *ban* on keeping handguns and functional firearms in the home for self-defense is unreasonable and unconstitutional under any standard.

But not in Obama's America.

For new, breaking information on Barack Obama since this book was published, please go to www.audacityofdeceit.com. If you have friends who would like to receive this chapter, or any of the chapters in this book, please refer them to the same Web site where they can download the chapter of their choice for free.

CHAPTER THREE

VOTING RIGHTS TURNED UPSIDE DOWN

"It hasn't escaped notice that the felon vote would prove a windfall for the Democrats; when they do get to vote, convicts and ex-cons tend to pull the lever for the Left. Had ex-felons been able to vote in Florida in 2000—the state permanently strips all felons of voting rights—Al Gore almost certainly would have won the presidential election."[1]

—Edward Feser

I MAGINE TWO young men, both from the same neighborhood in Des Moines, Iowa, graduating from the same high school on the same day in June of 1997.

One enlists in the U.S. Army and is selected for Officer Candidate School. After several years in the service, he attains the rank of captain. In June 2007, ten years after high school graduation, he's now serving his third tour of duty in the Iraq War, leading an infantry company of more than 160 men.

The other fellow gets involved with drugs and becomes an addict. He can't hold down a regular job and, arrested for drug dealing, receives a slap on the wrist. But, when he robs a convenience store at gunpoint, he goes to prison for three years. In June 2007, ten years after high school graduation, he finally completes his five years of post-release probation.

Six months later, in January 2008, one of the most important events of the nation's presidential primary season—the Iowa Caucuses—takes place across the state. But only one of these young men is permitted to make his voice heard in choosing America's next president. The other, because of the decisions he made after graduating from high school, is barred from participating in the process.

But surprisingly, the *soldier* is the one excluded from the primary process. The ex-felon is welcomed into the caucus meeting room, where he is allowed to cast his caucus vote for Barack Obama to become America's next president and commander-in-chief of our armed forces. The other young man, risking his life to serve his country in a war zone half a world away from his home and family, is denied the right to voice his vote.

The story of these particular two men is fictional. But the facts are real.

In the 2008 primary cycle, servicemembers from Iowa and nine other caucus states were denied their right to participate in choosing our next president. Yet, thanks to an executive order signed by former Iowa governor Tom Vilsack, the state's felons who had completed their prison and parole terms were warmly welcomed to the caucuses. Not surprisingly, Obama won all but one of these states' caucuses.

Had Obama wanted military participation, the outcome of the caucuses in these ten states could have been different. Three states considered it a civil rights violation to deny the right to vote to military men and women serving in Iraq and Afghanistan, and these states made provisions to ensure that these Americans' rights were not violated. But, needless to say, the suppression of the military vote in other states was just fine with Barack Obama.

In Barack Obama's America, this upside-down logic in voting rights between convicted felons and our military servicemembers would not be remedied. That's bad enough. But, in fact, this topsy-turvy strategy would dramatically expand.

Mistreating Combat Vets

Barack Obama has done nothing to ensure that the votes of our military men and women are counted. He has even refused to co-sponsor pending U.S. Senate legislation designed to safeguard the votes of our military personnel.

In fact, Barack Obama has never distinguished himself as a supporter of our troops. Although other U.S. senators disagreed with President Bush's decision to pursue the war in Iraq, even some of the staunchest opponents of the war have spent a great deal of time visiting the troops, listening to their views, and making sure that they and their families get the support they need, overseas and here at home.

The same cannot be said for Barack Obama. As Pete Hegseth reported June 5, 2008 in the *Wall Street Journal*, "Since his election to the United States Senate in 2004, Mr. Obama has traveled to Iraq just once—in January 2006. This was more than a year before General David Petraeus took command and the surge began. It was also several months before Prime Minister Nouri al-Maliki's government came into office. Although Mr. Obama frequently criticizes the Iraqi leader on the campaign trail, he has never actually met him."[2]

Hegseth continues: "Even more astonishing than Mr. Obama's absence from Iraq, however, is the fact that he has apparently never sought out a single one-on-one meeting with General Petraeus. The general has made repeated trips back to Washington, but Mr. Obama has shown no interest in meeting privately with him."

In short, though he desires to become America's commander-in-chief, Obama didn't show any inclination to travel abroad and meet with our troops—not the enlisted men and women serving in the field nor with our top commander in the Iraq theater—until quite late in his presidential bid. While Obama did eventually go to Iraq and meet with Petraeus, this was not until *after* the primaries, after he became the presumptive Democratic nominee.

An aspiring commander-in-chief should be concerned about the issues facing wounded veterans, but sadly, Obama hasn't shown the desire to meet with returning troops, either. In fact, in April 2005, Sergeant Garrett Anderson—wounded in Iraq while serving with the Illinois National Guard—traveled with twelve other combat veterans to meet with his Illinois senator, Barack Obama, in Washington, D.C. Obama refused to give these veterans even one minute of his time. Obama's Senate staff made it clear that the senator had no intention of meeting with them.[3] He sent them back to Illinois, without ever looking them in the eye. Needless to say, this is strange behavior for a United States presidential candidate.

Given Obama's attitude toward soldiers and veterans, it comes as no surprise that he has thus far refused to sign on as a co-sponsor of S. 3073, also known as the "Military Voting Protection Act of 2008," now pending in the U.S. Senate. This bill, along with companion legislation in the House of Representatives, was introduced based on Congressional findings that "the ability of the members of the armed forces to vote while serving overseas has been hampered by numerous factors, including inadequate processes for ensuring their timely receipt of absentee ballots, delivery methods that are typically slow and antiquated, and a myriad of voting procedures that are often confusing…." In addition, Congress found that members of our armed forces and other U.S. citizens overseas requested almost one million absentee ballots in 2006, but less than one-third of these were received by local election officials.

The voting problems are indeed bad for our 175,000 troops in Iraq and Afghanistan, and it is little wonder that Obama and liberal Democrats refuse to help these American heroes who historically vote against them. In fact, eleven states in the U.S. hold primaries for state offices in September and October, which causes delays in absentee ballot mailings even to residents of these states.

Private organizations and foundations have tried to help remedy this problem. For example, FedEx and the Overseas Vote Foundation just unveiled a speedier process that unfortunately is very costly. The delivery service can pick up ballots and return them within one to five days for a fee of $23.50. Voters can also use the organization's Web site to apply for a ballot—significantly quickening a process that normally takes weeks for military voters.

Often, if military ballots aren't received by a certain date, they aren't counted at all, as those who tally the votes consider the process too cumbersome and time-consuming.

The Military Voting Protection Act of 2008 seeks to remedy this grave injustice against the volunteers who serve our country abroad in the Army, Navy, Air Force, Marine Corps, Coast Guard, and National Guard. But just as he has so far refused to meet with America's soldiers and veterans, Barack Obama has similarly turned up his nose at this urgently needed Senate legislation.

LET THE INMATES RUN THE ASYLUM

Make no mistake. Barack Obama *is* interested in expanding voting "rights." Indeed, he is the proud co-sponsor of another Senate bill—the deceptively labeled "Count Every Vote Act," introduced by Hillary Clinton of New York—that would expand voting rights to up to five million citizens.

Most of these Americans haven't served in Iraq. In fact, most have never served one day in the military, and probably never will. But they have one thing in common: They have all been convicted of felonies in our courts of law—felonies that range all the way up to rape, armed robbery, and murder.

So, while Obama has taken affirmative steps to restore voting rights to convicts, who are guilty of rape, murder, child molestation, and other heinous felonies, after they are released from prison, he would not even sign on to the bill to ensure that servicemembers are able to vote. In Barack Obama's world, our military heroes will continue to be denied their rights, while convicted felons—including those who used deadly weapons to threaten or harm their fellow citizens—will enjoy full benefits of citizenship, including participating in choosing America's presidents and other elected officials.

Laws that govern felons' voting rights vary from state to state. Prison inmates are barred from voting in every state but two. In thirty-three states, parolees are not allowed to vote. Persons serving probation are not allowed to vote in twenty-nine states. And, in most other states, felons lose their voting rights for life.

But Barack Obama wants the federal government to overturn all of these state laws, take the matter into its own hands, and *require* every state to restore voting rights to convicted felons on the same day they complete their prison terms and parole. Under this legislation, federal law would also require all fifty state governments to spend taxpayer dollars to notify convicted felons of their voting rights.

Proponents of restoring the right of felons to vote claim that there is no reason to bar these criminals from voting once they have "paid their debt to society." They say that fairness requires us to restore these criminals' rights.

But, as respected public policy researcher John R. Lott, Jr., has pointed out, convicted felons lose many other rights, not just the right to vote. For example, felons are not allowed to hold professional business licenses and are therefore barred from practicing law, medicine, and many other professions. They cannot work for the government. They may not serve as an officer in a publicly traded company. "In some cases," Lott observes, "felons can lose their right to inherit property, to collect pension benefits, or even to get a truck driving license."[4]

Not one senator has put forth a proposal to allow convicted criminals to practice medicine or law. Not one senator has put forth a proposal to allow or require the government to hire ex-cons. And not one senator has put forth a proposal to allow criminals to buy guns once they've completed their prison terms and parole. But according to Hillary Clinton and Barack Obama, these criminals—no matter how much damage they've done to law-abiding citizens—should be allowed to vote, and should have a full say in who runs our country in the years to come.

Consider the insight provided by Professor Edward Feser in addressing the issue of felon voting shortly after the last presidential election:

> If the right to vote is as precious as felon advocates claim to believe it is, we should expect people to uphold at least some minimum moral standards in order to keep it—such as refraining from violating their fellow voters' own inalienable rights.
>
> Those pushing for felon voting will thus need to come up with much better arguments before they can hope to convince their fellow citizens. They ought at least to try. People might otherwise begin to suspect that the hope of gaining political advantage is the only reason they advocate reform.[5]

Is it any coincidence that the list of co-sponsors to Clinton's bill reads like a "who's who" of gun-ban extremists in the Senate? The list includes not only Obama, but Senators Barbara Boxer of California, John Kerry of Massachusetts, and Frank Lautenberg of New Jersey. Every one of these senators has been a leading proponent of denying law-abiding citizens their Second Amendment right to keep and bear arms, whether through national gun registration, gun-owner licensing, ammo bans, or outright bans on the sale of firearms. (As described elsewhere in this book, Barack Obama supports shutting down every gun store within five miles of a school or park—a move that would immediately close an estimated 90 percent of gun stores in America.)

Yet, Obama wants to enhance the rights of those who use firearms in commission of a crime, by allowing these felons to exercise their "right" to vote. Why? He knows full well that if these criminals show up at the polls, most will vote for liberal, gun ban candidates such as himself, not for conservative candidates who support the right of law-abiding citizens to use firearms for the defense of their homes and loved ones. And Obama knows that, if enough felons cast their votes on Election Day, he and his fellow gun -ban extremists can win the power they need to overturn our Second Amendment rights, once and for all.

According to Clinton's "Count Every Vote Act" itself, Clinton's "Count Every Vote Act" legislation would restore voting rights to up to 5.4 million convicted felons. But despite its lofty title—and despite Congress's findings that red tape and delays routinely deny our military personnel *their* right to vote—the bill does nothing to restore voting rights for veterans.

In its entire 117 pages of text, the bill mentions the word "veterans" only once, in order to make it clear that veterans shall not be denied their right to vote, *provided that they have been convicted of at least one felony.* For the millions of veterans and active duty personnel who have never been convicted of a crime, this bill does *absolutely nothing* to secure their right to vote in any future election.

As American voters consider their choices for the next president of the United States—and for the next commander-in-chief of our armed forces—we need to ask ourselves some very important questions.

Does America want a president who considers the votes of felons more important than the votes of our overseas military personnel?

Does America want a president who would restore voting "rights" to millions of criminals, while refusing to support an effort to ensure that our volunteer servicemembers overseas can participate in the democratic process by casting *their* ballots?

When Barack Obama says "every vote should count," he means that every vote cast by *his* constituency should count. In co-sponsoring a bill on behalf of felons's voting rights and refusing to support corresponding legislation for military voters,

Obama demonstrates that the rights and votes of convicted felons are worth more to him than those of Americans who serve in our military. This is an appalling contradiction from a man who would be president of the United States.

But, in Barack Obama's America, those who murder, rape, or molest their fellow citizens will be allowed the same rights as law-abiding citizens when it comes to deciding who should govern our country and make our laws. At the same time—in Barack Obama's America—those who volunteer to serve in our armed services and defend our freedoms overseas will continue to be denied their full right to participate in the American political process.

For new, breaking information on Barack Obama since this book was published, please go to www.audacityofdeceit.com. If you have friends who would like to receive this chapter, or any of the chapters in this book, please refer them to the same Web site where they can download the chapter of their choice for free.

CHAPTER FOUR

WAR ON SUCCESS

"On fiscal policy, both Barack Obama and Hillary Clinton want higher taxes.... On trade, they oppose new free-trade agreements and want to renegotiate NAFTA *with Canada and Mexico.*

"As it happens, another president embraced such policies in a time of economic slowdown and financial market turbulence. Herbert Hoover raised taxes on high earners sharply and...signed the Smoot-Hawley [trade] tariff in 1930. The results were not pretty. Until now, his example has not commended itself to Democrats."[1]

—Author and *U.S. News and World Report* senior writer Michael Barone

U NDER *BARACK OBAMA'S* tax policy, if you work hard, invest your time and money wisely, and make a million dollars in 2009, you will get to keep $455,000 and hand over more than half (54.5 percent) of your earnings to the federal government. Then, state and local governments get to pick your pocket, too.

On the other hand, if you are lucky and win a million dollars in a state-sponsored lottery, on which Americans annually spend more than $45 billion, you will also pay 54.5 percent of your winnings—or $545,000—in federal taxes.[2]

Does this sound fair?

THE AMERICAN DREAM

Each year over one million people legally become American citizens.[3] One of the reasons why so many people from scores of other nations come to the United States is because our country offers so much promise for a better life, a life free from prosecution and persecution. For over one hundred years they have come—grandparents and parents of many present-day Americans—to the land of opportunity. Deep in our common American heritage is the belief that if you work or study hard, anyone can become the next Henry Ford, Bill Gates, George Washington Carver, Alexander Graham Bell, Sally Ride, or Margaret Mead. These great men and women—and many more like them—have contributed so much to the American Dream, making our lives easier, more successful, and more fulfilling. Their successes have attracted millions of people from all over the world to America, including people who believe you can get lucky and strike it rich.

Successful generations have created the world's number-one economy—by far. Even when shades of recession struck in the spring of 2008, the gross domestic product (GDP)—the value of all goods and services produced and sold in the U.S.—was still measured at a whopping $13.8 *trillion*.[4] No other country comes close.

But, if Barack Obama is allowed to set the nation's economic policies and priorities, he will throw a wrench into the gears of this remarkable economic machine and America will face a new war. Call it Obama's "war on success."

To the casual observer, Obama appears to "get it," and seems to recognize that America's economic model has been wildly successful—even through periods of diminished economic activity. But, like so much of the candidate's eloquent rhetoric, his comprehension seems superficial and limited to his campaign speeches.

In practice, rather than seeking to protect and preserve our successful economic model, Obama seems obsessed with tearing it down and replacing it with a government-focused "solution," one that has a well-established history of failure. We have every indication that Obama will likely punish success, confiscating wealth and redistributing it to those who have neither earned it nor deserved it. Quite simply, Obama will raise taxes—a lot. This will be especially so for those Americans who have the audacity to emulate the successes of their fathers, grandfathers, and forefathers.

Completing a questionnaire for the Independent Voters of Illinois/Independence Precinct Organization (IVI/IPO), Obama elaborated on his left-wing views and "progressive" agenda. To the question, "Do you support (b) maintaining the current corporate/individual [tax] ratio?" Obama answered, "I strongly favor a graduated income tax for both individuals and corporations that would shift an increasing burden on corporations and individuals most able to pay."[5]

In fact, Obama has outlined ten specific tax changes to which he will subject Americans. They are:

1) Increase the top individual tax rate from 35 percent to 39.6 percent.

2) Raise the capital gains tax rate from 15 percent to 28 percent.

3) Increase the stock dividends rate from 15 percent to 39.6 percent.

4) Raise the percentage of Americans who pay no federal income tax from 40 percent to 50 percent.

5) Impose a 10 percent surtax on all incomes above $250,000 per year.

6) Raise the death tax rate to 55 percent for any income past the first $1 million exemption.

7) Raise the minimum wage from $6.55 to $9.50

8) Raise social security payments by 4 percent for individuals, businesses, or anyone who makes $250,000 per year.

9) Increase the top tax rate from 37.9 percent to 54.9 percent for self-employed taxpayers (who already pay ordinary income taxes as well as self-employment taxes).

10) Increase the tax rate on Subchapter S-corporations (small businesses) by up to 15.3 percent (from a top rate of 35 percent to 50.3 percent).

Obama's plan is not only confiscatory and authoritarian, but regressive. For example, in addition to all the new taxes, he would roll back the tax cuts passed by Congress during the Bush administration. Further, his plan would cost Americans far more in taxes than they paid during the Clinton administration—another Democratic regime that imposed, at the time, the nation's largest tax hike, in 1993.

Unfortunately, it should be easy for Obama to raise our taxes. Like Democrat Lyndon Johnson, Obama may well enjoy working majorities in Congress. Democrats currently hold 236 seats in the House of Representatives and expect to gain at least ten to thirty seats. In the Senate, they look to gain at least four to seven seats to add to their current majority of fifty-one senators.[6] Under Johnson, individual tax rates soared to 70 percent, and the capital gains tax was an oppressive 50 percent.[7] As a result, the country suffered a weak economy that was more susceptible to major and even minor disruptions.

On the other hand, since Ronald Reagan lowered the top tax rate in 1986 to 28 percent, we have weathered a stock market crash in 1987; financial meltdowns in Mexico in 1994; a major economic downturn in Asia in 1997; the collapse of long-term capital management in 1998; the September 11, 2001, terrorist attacks; and the dot-com bust. Low tax rates gave our economy the resiliency it needed to overcome crisis.

Of course, our strong economy generates trillions of dollars and produces tens of millions of jobs. Even during some economic weakening in early 2008, the U.S. unemployment rate stood at 5.5 percent in May 2008.[8] Compare this to the high unemployment rate in the European Union (6.7 percent), and individual EU member nations such as Spain (9.6 percent), France (8.1 percent), and Germany (7.6 percent).[9]

THE PRICE WE WILL PAY

According to an analysis by the Heritage Foundation, when Obama allows the Bush tax cuts to expire, he "will discourage investment and slow economic growth."[10] Specifically, the Foundation estimates the higher taxes on capital gains and dividends will lead to a net job loss of 270,000 job in 2011 and another 413,000 jobs in 2018. "Similar job losses continue for the next seven years of our model's forecast horizon of 2008 through 2018." Similarly, economic output as measured by gross domestic product (GDP) after inflation would fall by $44 billion in 2011 and $50 billion in 2012, from the levels that the economy would attain without this policy change. "These economic effects would be vividly evident in take-home pay. Personal income after taxes would decline by $113 billion after inflation in 2011 and $133 billion after inflation in 2012 when compared, again, to levels that would likely prevail without tax rates going back up."[11]

Of course, to balance job losses (and pander to workers), Obama's plan includes a hefty increase in the minimum wage—a whopping 45 percent! While it does little to help those who've lost their jobs, the increase will hurt every retail store, gas station, dry cleaners, grocery store, and other small businesses—as well as large ones.

Certainly, Obama's planned tax increases are nothing new from a Democrat. It's also not new to couple these tax hikes with increases in free trade barriers—as Obama also plans. This dangerously toxic recipe, in fact, mirrors the policy failures of President Herbert Hoover's administration. And they left a bad taste in America's mouth.

"It's usually government actions that cause destructive economic troubles and excesses," wrote Steve Forbes in 2008. "The Great Depression, for instance, is always cited as *prima facie* proof as to why we need active government involvement. To the contrary, government blundering brought on the disaster, starting with [Hoover's] Smoot-Hawley Tariff of 1929-30, which began a devastating trade war that, in turn, dried up international trade and flows of global capital. That horrible error was compounded in the U.S. by Herbert Hoover's massive tax increase [from a top rate of 25 percent to 63 percent] to balance the budget in 1932. Hoover thought a balanced budget would revive confidence. Instead, the deficit ballooned, as the high taxes deepened the slump."[12]

The lesson of Herbert Hoover is that the ability to tax excessively is the ability to destroy the economy. Apparently, Barack Obama didn't learn that lesson at Harvard.

And Obama has another tax trick up his sleeve—raising the capital gains tax. Unfortunately, this element of his tax proposal would cost even more jobs—and worse—as it would bring capital spending to a grinding halt. Investors would lose confidence that their investments in new plants and jobs would turn a profit. With high taxes, foreign investors would look elsewhere, and flock to emerging markets outside the U.S. So the winners under Obama's tax policies will not likely be American workers, but workers and corporations in eastern Europe, China, India, and Brazil.

And, on the American side, it won't be just labor and the "rich" who are hurt by a capital gains tax hike. Fifty percent of households earning less than $50,000 report capital gains on their income tax returns, and 79 percent of those earning $100,000 or less take a capital gains discount.[13] Today, roughly half of all American households—57 million of them—are invested in the stock market.[14]

Does any of this sound like the "change" Barack Obama has planned for you?

MAKING 40 PERCENT PAY FOR ALL

Interestingly, Obama's strategy *would* reduce some Americans' tax burdens. No, these reductions are not for those who already pay their "fair share," (or more than their fair share), but for those who do not. Indeed, the liberal Democrat from Illinois has talked explicitly about redistributing America's wealth to reach the needy.

Currently, 32 percent of all Americans who file a tax return pay no federal income tax but receive credits, handouts, and deductions.[15] But, Obama's plan provides $100 billion in tax credits, and the percentage of tax filers who do not pay any income tax would rise from 32 percent to roughly 40 percent of the U.S. population, absolving an additional 8 percent of American tax filers of their federal income tax responsibility.[16] Obama's tax law would provide senior citizen tax credits, college credits, childcare credits, home buyer credits, and $1,000-per-family credits. With all that he has to offer, unfortunately, Obama's redistributionist schemes would make our tax forms even more complex and confusing, adding insult to injury.

Riding for free, nearly half of America will consume a majority of government handouts and services, while the other half foots the entire bill and covers the entire cost of government. Of course, nobody likes to pay taxes. But responsible Americans recognize that our society needs to fund a government that can provide roads and bridges, airports, a functional infrastructure, and a strong defense.

Taxes are a fact of life, but *all* Americans should do their part, contribute an equal share, based on income, to support our country and pay for services. Not so, for Barack Obama's "vision" of change in America. He seeks to punish our most enterprising and successful citizens—those who create companies, hire workers, and pay benefits—by making them pay for everything else, too, while 40 percent of Americans use the government's benefits and services for free.

That is certainly not *fair*, and it's not the kind of principle our Founding Fathers envisioned when they created a nation in which the central government represents everyone and, hence, is supported by everyone. Furthermore, they certainly did not envision a nation divided by pandering politicians who, in their selfish bid for higher office, create disunity, pitting one group against another just to get votes. With America's great diversity, we have always seen populations of people of greater and lesser means, greater and lesser ambition, greater and lesser success. For the most part, America is still the land of opportunity, and most Americans can still—as always—achieve their goals. But it helps if government doesn't stand in the way.

In the last century, communism was tested and it failed. In this great experiment, communist and socialist governments—not the people or the businesses themselves—determined wages, prices, fees, and taxes. The result: These countries are among the world's poorest, because their people have no incentive to perform, excel, do well, create more, grow more, work harder or more efficiently, become better educated, or invest more. Worse, their governments remain repressive and unfair. Without oppression, communism and socialism cannot work, and it will certainly not work in America. But with heavy taxation of the "rich" and his class warfare mentality, this is the direction of Obama's "change" for America.

"US VS. THEM"

Obama has complained that congressional tax cuts have led to fewer taxes for the wealthy. In fact, his rhetoric even vilifies those in our highest tax bracket, treating "wealth" like a dirty word. This view is not only contemptuous and divisive, but destructive and misleading. The truth is that those Americans earning the most money have steadily paid *more*–not less—income tax throughout recent years.

For example, the non-partisan Tax Foundation examined Internal Revenue Service tax data. According to their study:

> The truth is that the vast majority of federal income taxes are paid by high-income earners. According to the most recent IRS data available, the top 10 percent of households—with incomes roughly $100,000 or greater—pay roughly 70 percent of all federal income taxes. That share is up from just below 50 percent in 1980...

> But just because a couple's combined salaries seem high doesn't make them wealthy. For example, a young factory worker earning $18 an hour—or $36,700 per year—clearly falls into the statistical middle. But if she marries a man earning the same amount, their combined income of $73,400 is enough to qualify them to be in the top 20 percent of Americans.[17]

Further facts clearly demonstrate this:

- The number of households earning $100,000 or more annually nearly doubled over the past twenty years (22.2 million households in 2006 vs. 11.6 million in 1986).[18]

- The number of households earning $35,000 or less has changed only marginally over the past twenty years, by 17 percent.[19]

- Many of those who left the $35,000 bracket moved into higher income brackets (many of them joining the $100,000 and above income bracket).

- Many of those who left the $35,000 bracket were replaced by some of the 19.5 million legal immigrants who arrived in our country over the last twenty years,[20] and more than 19 million Americans who graduated from high school but did not pursue a college degree.[21]

Most Americans feel confident and optimistic about the opportunity that this great nation affords them, believing they have plenty of potential to earn a median income.

Such optimism and desire for advancement is borne out by the fact that 82 percent of Americans graduate from high school[22] and 67 percent of high school graduates pursue a college degree.[23] The number of Americans striving for higher education is especially striking when compared to 1960, when only 45 percent of American high school graduates pursued college.[24] Also, only 65 percent of French students and 43 percent of students in Spain graduate from high school, and a paltry 46 percent and 33 percent, respectively, pursue a college degree.[25] Many Americans invest in higher education because they believe they will have the opportunity to prosper financially.

Despite this fundamental and pervasive belief, Barack Obama wants to take America off our Founding Fathers' path of freedom and prosperity and lead us down a different road, one on which the federal government—widely believed to be an inept manager of the taxpayers' money—increases its voracious monetary appetite and forces us to pay more in homage. King George III practiced exactly this kind of fiscal tyranny.

Not surprisingly, most Americans oppose tax hikes. A 2007 Gallup poll found that a clear majority of Americans felt they pay "too much" in federal income taxes, while only 2 percent thought their federal income taxes were too low.[26] In fact, 75 percent of Americans believe millionaires should pay no more than 30 percent of their income in federal taxes.[27] Americans don't want taxes raised on the wealthy, because they believe that they can achieve wealth in the future, and they don't want to be punished for their hard work and success. In addition, all too many Americans remember what the federal government's heavy hand under Presidents Johnson and Carter did to economic growth and the American standard of living.

Demanding that the rich must pay their "fair share," Obama expresses class warfare rhetoric that plays well with certain voters, but this demand is as dishonest as it is misguided. In fact, the wealthiest 1 percent of our population generates 19 percent of our country's total income, but they pay *39 percent of all income taxes.*[28] And the top 10 percent pay *68 percent* of the tab. By contrast, the bottom half of wage earners bring in 13 percent of total income *but only pay 3 percent of all income taxes.*[29] This group, Obama says, pays too much and deserves a bigger break.

Obama's plan will punish the most successful people in our country by confiscating their wealth and that of their companies. But even this is devious. His plan changes the provisions for Subchapter S-corporations, increasing the top tax rate to 50.3 percent. These corporations include many of America's small businesses, and this provision will in fact raise the tax burden of almost 3.3 million small businesses in America.

RAISING TAXES EASY FOR OBAMA

When President Reagan cut the top tax rate from 70 to 28 percent, he initiated an impressive era of growth and wealth creation. Today, thousands of Americans could invest hard work and dedication and finally "strike it rich.," We enjoy the American Dream because our hard work pays off.

But the Dream may well turn into a nightmare if Barack Obama wins the White House, with sympathetic Democrats in both the House and Senate. With one-party control of government—the executive branch, Congress, and eventually the courts—Obama and his policies will lead America headlong into economic stagnation, double-digit inflation, government price controls, gas lines, and 10 percent unemployment.

Often compared to John F. Kennedy, Barack Obama, like millions of Americans, makes no secret of his admiration for the enormously popular Democratic president. But Obama would do well to recall the following from President Kennedy's State of the Union Address of January 14, 1963:

[I]t is increasingly clear—to those in government, business, and labor who are responsible for our economy's success—that our obsolete tax system exerts too heavy a drag on private purchasing power, profits, and employment…. It discourages extra effort and risk. It distorts the use of resources. It invites recurrent recessions, depresses our federal revenues, and causes chronic budget deficits.

Despite his elegant oratory style, Barack Obama is no Jack Kennedy. Obama has never run a business, but spent most of his adult life politicking and pandering to far-left constituencies. Obama is in fact more like Herbert Hoover than Jack Kennedy; Obama will likely raise taxes, redistribute wealth, and discourage both investment and achievement. In Obama's America, "change" is not something we want to believe in.

For new, breaking information on Barack Obama since this book was published, please go to www.audacityofdeceit.com. If you have friends who would like to receive this chapter, or any of the chapters in this book, please refer them to the same Web site where they can download the chapter of their choice for free.

CHAPTER FIVE

BANKRUPTING AMERICA

"Obama's economic doctrine subsidizes people who make wrong decisions and does little to encourage them to make the right ones. Failure becomes an option, the flip side of success. One can make money either way."[1]

—Cal Thomas, *Insight Magazine*

THE KEY TO RONALD REAGAN'S success was not just lowering taxes, but also cutting spending. We haven't got a prayer that this will be the legacy of a Barack Obama presidency. Along with international environmentalists and third-world countries, Obama apparently believes that 35 percent of Americans can afford tax rates that add up to 54 percent, all to pay for his expensive domestic and international programs.

Part of the problem is that Obama's spend-a-thon doesn't stop at America's borders. As the author of the Global Poverty Act in the U.S. Senate, Obama proposes to tax seven-tenths of a percent of GDP in order to fund his $845 billion giveaway to the poor nations of the world. This is equal to all the federal taxes collected in the U.S. for a period of *four months*.[2] Obama's legislation does not reveal specifics on which countries would receive this aid, nor how much they would receive, because he turns that decision making over to the United Nations (U.N.). Using the U.N.'s development-expenditure statistics, we can assume that Africa would receive 47 percent of the aid, followed by 25 percent for Asia and 10 percent for South America. That is, if the money doesn't disappear under U.N. corruption and waste.

By any measure, Obama is among the biggest spenders in the Senate. Every year, the National Taxpayers Union (NTU) rates U.S. congressmen on their actual votes on every piece of legislation that significantly affects taxes, spending, debt, and regulatory burdens on consumers and taxpayers. The NTU gave Obama an "F" grade in 2006 and 2007. He is officially a "Big Spender."[3]

Another taxpayer watchdog group, Citizens Against Government Waste (CAGW), also rates the congressional votes of our legislators in an effort to separate the taxpayer advocates from those who indulge in wasteful or pork-barrel spending. CAGW's 2006 ratings, the most current ratings available from the group at the time this book was going to print, show that Obama received a score of 30 on a scale of 0 to 100, in which 0 is "Hostile" to taxpayers and 100 is a "Taxpayer SuperHero." Obama's score places him firmly in the category of "Unfriendly" to taxpayers.

Obama's spending plans, proposals, and legislation illustrate the demerits of his big-spending liberal policies and speak for themselves. For example, the Independent Voters of Illinois/Independence Precinct Organization (IVI/IPO) posed the question, "Do you support (b) workfare?"

"I oppose arbitrary time limits or work requirements that fail to take into account the lack of entry level jobs," Obama responded. "I do favor measures that would expand child care...transportation subsidies, and sustained job training that actually encourage welfare recipients to enter the workforce."[4]

To the question, "What is your position on...raising the minimum wage?" he answered, "I support raising the minimum wage to assure that any employee working full-time enjoys a livable wage."[5]

The National Taxpayers' Union conducted an analysis of Obama's spending proposals. The following are their descriptions and the estimated costs associated with Obama's biggest spending programs:[6]

ECONOMIC STIMULUS PACKAGE

"Barack Obama's economic plan will inject $75 billion of stimulus into the economy by getting money in the form of tax cuts and direct spending directly to the people who need it most.

"Obama's proposal will immediately provide stimulus using means that do not require lengthy governmental or administrative delays....

"Obama is calling for providing middle- and low-income seniors—who would not benefit from the workers' tax credit—an immediate, one-time $250 supplement to their Social Security benefit.... These payments would not alter the Social Security program and would not use revenue from the Social Security trust funds.... Obama's plan will provide $10 billion in immediate relief to the states and localities hardest hit by the housing crisis....

"Obama is calling for a temporary expansion of the UI [Unemployment Insurance] program for those who have exhausted their current eligibility. Obama also believes that the extension of UI benefits should be coupled with an expansion of UI eligibility to more workers, including many part-time and non-traditional workers who are currently left out of the program. Stimulus: $10 billion."[7]

Cost: $30 billion (first-year cost)

WELFARE—EARNED INCOME TAX CREDIT

"As president, Obama will reward work by increasing the number of working parents eligible for EITC benefits, increasing the benefit available to parents who support their children through child support payments, and reducing the EITC marriage penalty which hurts low-income families. Under the Obama plan, full-time workers making minimum wage would get an EITC benefit up to $555, more than three times greater than the $175 benefit they get today. If the workers are responsibly supporting their children on child support, the Obama plan would give those workers a benefit of $1,110. Obama would also increase the EITC benefit for those families most likely to be in poverty—families with three or more children."[8]

Cost: $2.64 billion per year

LABOR—"MAKING WORK PAY" REFUNDABLE TAX CREDIT

"Barack Obama will restore fairness to the Tax Code and provide 150 million workers the tax relief they deserve. Obama will create a new 'Making Work Pay' tax credit of up to $500 per person, or $1,000 per working family. This refundable income tax credit will provide direct relief to American families who face the regressive payroll tax system. It will offset the payroll tax on the first $8,100 of their earnings while still preserving the important principle of a dedicated revenue source for Social Security. The 'Making Work Pay' tax credit will completely eliminate income taxes for 10 million Americans. The tax credit will also provide relief to self-employed small business owners who struggle to pay both the employee and employer portion of the payroll tax. The 'Making Work Pay' tax credit offsets some of this self-employment tax as well."[9]

Cost: $61.6 billion per year

HEALTHCARE PLAN

"Specifically, the Obama plan will: (1) establish a new public insurance program, available to Americans who neither qualify for Medicaid or SCHIP nor have access to insurance through their employers, as well as to small businesses that want to offer insurance to their employees; (2) create a National Health Insurance Exchange to help Americans and businesses that want to purchase private health insurance directly; (3) require all employers to contribute towards health coverage for their employees or towards the cost of the public plan; (4) mandate all children have healthcare coverage; (5) expand eligibility for the Medicaid and SCHIP programs; and (6) allow flexibility for state health reform plans.... The Obama plan will improve efficiency and lower costs in the healthcare system by: (1) offering federal reinsurance to employers to help ensure that unexpected or catastrophic illnesses do not make health insurance unaffordable or out of reach for businesses and their employees (2) ensuring that patients receive and providers deliver the best possible care; (3) adopting state-of-the-art health information technology systems; and (4) reforming our market structure to increase competition."

Cost: $65 billion per year[10]

MEDICARE PRESCRIPTION DRUG BENEFIT "DOUGHNUT HOLE"

"Barack Obama will...Fix Medicare's Prescription Drug 'Doughnut Hole.' Barack Obama wants to close the 'doughnut hole' in the Medicare Part D Prescription Drug Program that limits benefits for seniors with more than $2,250 but less than $5,100 in annual drug costs."[11]

Cost: $29.573 billion per year

MEDICAID—COMMUNITY-BASED ATTENDANT SERVICES

"Barack Obama supports efforts to ensure that this program remains solvent. He believes that the federal government should support state-level reform efforts to constrain Medicaid costs such as negotiating for low drug prices, implementing disease management and quality initiatives, and offering greater support for community-based, long-term care services. Obama would also reverse cuts in benefits or changes in eligibility that prevent low-income patients from seeking care until their medical problems have gotten worse and more expensive to treat."[12]

Cost: $5.4 billion per year

HOUSING—FORECLOSURE PREVENTION FUND

"Obama will create a fund to help people refinance their mortgages and provide comprehensive supports to innocent homeowners. The fund will also assist individuals who purchased homes that are simply too expensive for their income levels by helping to sell their homes. The fund will help offset costs of selling a home, including helping low-income borrowers get additional time and support to pay back any losses from the sale of their home and waiving certain federal, state, and local income taxes that result from an individual selling their home to avoid foreclosure."

Cost: $10 billion (first year cost)

HOUSING—UNIVERSAL MORTGAGE REFUNDABLE CREDIT

"Barack Obama will ensure that anyone with a mortgage, not just the well-off, can take advantage of this tax incentive for homeownership by creating a universal mortgage credit. This 10 percent credit will benefit an additional 10 million homeowners, the majority of whom earn less than $50,000 per year. Non-itemizers will be eligible for this refundable credit, which will provide the average recipient with approximately $500 per year in tax savings. This tax credit will also help homeowners deal with the uncertain state of the housing market today."[13]

Cost: $4.4 billion per year

COMMUNITY DEVELOPMENT BLOCK GRANT (CDBG):

"The important Community Development Block Grant program, which provides urban areas with block grants to innovate and provide a full range of housing, job training, and community development services, has been cut by an astonishing 31 percent since Bush took office....

Barack Obama...will restore funding for the CDBG program."[14]

Cost: $1.693 billion (first-year cost)

EARLY EDUCATION AND K-12 PLAN

"Barack Obama's early education and K-12 plan package costs about $18 billion per year."[15]

Cost: $18 billion per year

EARLY LEARNING

"His comprehensive 'Zero to Five' plan will provide critical supports to young children and their parents by investing $10 billion per year to:

- Create Early Learning Challenge Grants to stimulate and help fund state 'zero to five' efforts.

- Quadruple the number of eligible children for Early Head Start, increase Head Start funding and improve quality for both. Work to ensure all children have access to pre-school.

- Provide affordable and high-quality child care that will promote child development and ease the burden on working families.

- Create a Presidential Early Learning Council to increase collaboration and program coordination across federal, state, and local levels."[16]

Cost: $10 billion per year

EDUCATION—PELL GRANTS

"Obama will work to ensure that the maximum Pell Grant award is increased for low income students by ensuring that the award keeps pace with the rising cost of inflation."[17]

Cost: $7.08 billion per year

EDUCATION—AMERICAN OPPORTUNITY TAX CREDIT

"Barack Obama will make college affordable for all Americans by creating a new American Opportunity Tax Credit. This universal and fully refundable credit will ensure that the first $4,000 of a college education is completely free for most Americans, and will cover two-thirds of the cost of tuition at the average public college or university. And by making the tax credit fully refundable, Obama's credit will help low-income families that need it the most. Obama will also ensure that the tax credit is available to families at the time of enrollment by using prior year's tax data to deliver the credit at the time that tuition is due, rather than a year or more later when tax returns are filed."[18]

Cost: $5.795 billion per year

TEACHING SERVICE SCHOLARSHIPS

"Barack Obama will create substantial, sustained Teaching Service Scholarships that completely cover training costs in high-quality teacher preparation or alternative certification programs at the undergraduate or graduate level for those who are willing to teach in a high-need field or location for at least four years.... Some Teaching Service Scholarships will be targeted to high-ability candidates who might not otherwise enter teacher preparation and the incentives will also be used proactively to recruit candidates to the fields and locations where they are needed. Nearly all of the vacancies currently filled with emergency teachers could be filled with talented, well-prepared teachers with 40,000 service scholarships of up to $25,000 each. The scholarships will cover four years of undergraduate or two years of graduate teacher education, including high-quality alternative programs for mid-career recruits in exchange for teaching for at least four years in [a] high-need field or location. The scholarships will be allocated on the basis of academic merit and other indicators of potential success in teaching and will be targeted to areas of teaching shortage as defined nationally and by individual states."[19]

Cost: $1 billion per year

WINDFALL ELIMINATION PROVISION (WEP) AND THE GOVERNMENT PENSION OFFSET (GPO)

"Protect the Social Security Benefits of Public Employees and their Families: Barack Obama cosponsored the Social Security Fairness Act, which would repeal the Windfall Elimination Provision and the Government Pension Offset. The first provision cuts the Social Security benefits of some public employees, while the second cuts the benefits of the spouse or widow of some public employees. These provisions hurt teachers, police officers, firefighters, and other public employees. Barack Obama believes that we have a responsibility to take care of workers who have devoted their lives to public service and that we shouldn't be discouraging our young people from working in these essential jobs."[20]

Cost: $5.17 billion per year

INFRASTRUCTURE—NEW ORLEANS HURRICANE PROTECTION SYSTEM

"Obama's comprehensive program to rebuild New Orleans and the Gulf Coast includes...[e]nsuring that New Orleans has a levee and pumping system to protect the city from a 100-year storm by 2011, with the ultimate goal of protecting the entire city from a Category 5 storm."[21]

Cost: $1.6 billion per year

POLLUTION CAP-AND-TRADE PROGRAM AND CLEAN ENERGY RESEARCH

"We must enact a cap[-]and[-]trade system that will dramatically reduce our carbon emissions."[22]

Cost: $56.48 billion per year

BORDER SECURITY AND IMMIGRATION REFORM

"Barack Obama wants to preserve the integrity of our borders. He supports additional personnel, infrastructure, and technology on the borders and at our ports of entry. Obama believes we need additional Customs and Border Protection agents equipped with better technology and real-time intelligence.[23]

"Barack Obama supports comprehensive immigration reform that includes improvement in our visa programs, including our legal permanent resident visa programs and temporary programs including the H-1B program, to attract some of the world's most talented people to America. We should allow immigrants who earn their degrees in the U.S. to stay, work, and become Americans over time. And we should examine our ability to increase the number of permanent visas we issue to foreign skilled workers. Obama will work to ensure immigrant workers are less dependent on their employers for their right to stay in the country and would hold accountable employers who abuse the system and their workers."[24]

Cost: $9.8 billion per year

Obama's *Blueprint for Change* outlines his many other major spending programs. You can visit www.ati-news.com for a link to a complete analysis of all of Obama's spending proposals.

While ratings from watchdog groups like the National Taxpayers Union and Citizens Against Government Waste reliably demonstrate Obama's spendthrift ways, they do not speak to the philosophical error of Obama's big-government mindset. Syndicated columnist Cal Thomas recently detailed those flaws:

> America was built on and sustained by a "can do" spirit.... Today, too many are taught a "can't do" spirit. They are told that because of factors over which they have no control—race, class, poverty—it is impossible for them to do anything for themselves and so they must increasingly rely on government. Government doesn't cure poverty. It merely sets up barriers that ensure that too many poor people will remain locked in

poverty. They are encouraged to vote for Democrats, if they want to keep receiving benefits.[25]

Obama's big-spending ways in the Senate and, now, his presidential spending proposals provide convincing evidence that the candidate offers nothing new, just an update of President Johnson's Great Society. If he has his way on taxation, trade, and spending, Obama's America will look a lot like the post-Depression era after President Franklin Roosevelt's New Deal.

For new, breaking information on Barack Obama since this book was published, please go to www.audacityofdeceit.com. If you have friends who would like to receive this chapter, or any of the chapters in this book, please refer them to the same Web site where they can download the chapter of their choice for free.

Chapter Six

STARVING AMERICA

"Obama is counting on the fact that many Americans have a poor grasp of history. He is counting on the fact that high gas prices and a slowing economy might tempt them to return to a philosophy that has failed repeatedly in the past. Have we forgotten the legacy of Lyndon Johnson and Jimmy Carter?....

The Carter administration was a time of long gas lines and rationing, stagflation and rising unemployment.... Rejecting the dynamism and innovation of America, Carter proposed that we simply learn to live with less.... Despite all of his charisma, Obama brings the same attitude."[1]

— *Townhall.com* columnist Richard H. Collins

BUNDANT, *AFFORDABLE* energy is the lifeblood of American prosperity and security. Energy nourishes our economy, fueling the small businesses, entrepreneurs, technological advancements, and healthcare innovations that generate the American standard of living—the envy of the world.

Considering the vital importance of energy, one would think a commonsense energy policy would be at the top of the federal government's priority list. Not so. Yet somehow, America has survived the energy policies of administrations that paid homage to the environmental lobby at the expense of our nation's energy security and freedom.

The results of inaction and failed policies of the past have, however, finally come home to roost. The rising price of gas at the pumps, as well as inflated home heating and cooling bills, pose an unthinkable dilemma for many Americans: *Should I buy groceries, or gas? Feed my family, or fill my tank so I can get to work?* Quite simply, we can no longer afford to turn a cold shoulder to our energy needs, and we must stop letting environmental lobbyists regulate our lives in the name of worshipping Mother Earth.

And that is why we cannot afford the presidency of Barack Obama.

If Obama is elected president, he will be so beholden to environmental lobbyists that he will not be able to change the doomed energy policies of the past. Make no mistake, those cheerleaders pounding the pavement for Obama's campaign are some of the most extreme characters of the environmental movement.

For example, Obama received a glowing endorsement from Friends of the Earth Action,[2] a radical anti-energy group founded by the late David Brower. Brower had an infamous disdain for human civilization and considered mankind a cancer on the Earth.

The group endorses Obama because of his "strong pro-environment record, his policy proposals, the profile he has given global warming in his campaign, and the broad mandate he is building for change."[3] Indeed, they endorse him because, like them, he is anti-energy and opposes increased production of American coal, oil, and gas. Also like them, Obama wants to spend billions of dollars speculating on unproven and unreliable renewable energy sources, such as ethanol, wind, and solar power, in hopes they will replace oil, coal, and nuclear energy by 2028.

Not surprisingly, Friends of the Earth Action supporters excitedly campaign for Barack Obama's presidency. After all, he shares their radical belief that Americans should be starved of the abundant energy that can be produced and consumed in the U.S., and even exported within the next ten years, particularly oil, coal, and nuclear power. Instead, Obama wants to spend our tax dollars to enrich American energy speculators in their ethanol, wind, and solar energy schemes.

Such alternative energy sources are woefully inadequate and incredibly expensive—and there is no scientific guarantee they will solve our energy problems, not now and not even thirty years from now.

OBAMA'S BAN ON OIL AND GAS PRODUCTION

The desolate, frozen tundra of the Arctic National Wildlife Refuge (ANWR) is approximately the size of South Carolina, spanning 19.6 million acres.[4] A small sliver of ANWR—only 0.01 percent of the entire refuge, a mere two thousand acres— roughly the size of Dulles International Airport—is projected to hold anywhere from 5.7 to 16 billions barrels of recoverable oil.[5] This is potentially enough oil to replace imported oil from the volatile Middle East for the next thirty years.[6] It is the most promising oil reserve since Prudhoe Bay. But even this will not pry Barack Obama from his apparent pledge of allegiance to the environmental lobby.

Obama voted in 2005 to ban any oil exploration in ANWR [7] and, even today, claims ANWR oil is not worth pursuing because it does not offer an immediate solution, as it would take ten years to get the oil from the region to to the marketplace.

Of course, this rhetoric is disingenuous. Even if ANWR's oil will not be available until 2019, we will still likely need it! But the shameful fact is that, in 1995, Bill Clinton vetoed congressional legislation to open ANWR to drilling. Had he signed that legislation, that oil would be flowing to our gas tanks right now, mitigating today's high cost of fuel.

Alarmingly, Obama appears to have learned nothing from Clinton's failed policy. Why? Obama has too many environmentalist supporters and, therefore, cannot pursue commonsense energy solutions. Instead, he must keep harping on the dubious promise of renewable energy.

ANWR isn't the only vital energy reserve to which Barack Obama wants to permanently restrict access. Again, reverting to the failed policies of the past, he also wants to ban oil and gas exploration off America's coast, an area commonly referred to as the Outer Continental Shelf (OCS).

In 1982, Congress began passing legislation that restricted more and more offshore areas from energy development. In 1990, President George H. W. Bush issued a presidential directive banning any new offshore oil and gas exploration. Eight years later, President Clinton extended these restrictions.[8] But, according to the U.S. Department of Interior, the OCS sits on 85.9 billion barrels of recoverable oil and 419.9 trillion cubic feet of natural gas.[9] That is enough oil and gas to heat 133 million homes for fifty years.[10] Unfortunately, it's not enough to encourage Barack Obama to part ways with the billion-dollar environmental lobby and its voters.

While Obama works to ensure that Americans can't touch this much-needed energy, Cuba and China are preparing to drill for oil and gas just off the coast of Florida.[11] Obama's refusal to support drilling in the OCS means that China (soon to be the world's largest consumer of oil) and Cuba (soon to be an exporter of *our* oil) will be able to harvest these vital resources right on America's doorstep, where American rigs should be drilling American oil for American consumers.

Fortunately, most Americans do not agree with Obama's plan to starve our nation of the oil and gas it needs. According to a May 2008 Gallup Poll, a clear majority of Americans, 57 percent, favor drilling for oil and gas off the U.S. coast and in wilderness areas such as ANWR. Only 41 percent (including Obama) are opposed to it.[12]

Ostensibly, Barack Obama has steadfastly refused to support the strategy the American people prefer, the strategy that is right for American consumers, the strategy that will secure our energy future and freedom. His is a minority ruling, driven by the campaign support of international environmental groups and their voters, who back him in his quest for the presidency.

FUELING THE HIGHWAY TO NOWHERE: ETHANOL

Few shams in the alternative-fuel industry are bigger than corn ethanol production, which diverts the billions of taxpayer dollars diverted to corn ethanol production. And few proponents of this speculator's dream have been more supportive than Barack Obama.

In December 2007, Obama championed and voted for a bill that will siphon 18 billion taxpayer dollars to the ethanol industry. On the stump, particularly in the Corn Belt, Obama never missed a chance to sing the praises of ethanol. However, his love for ethanol is is not just borne out of the fact that he is a senator from Illinois—a corn state.

When campaigning in farm country, Obama is often accompanied by his good buddy, former Senate majority leader Tom Daschle. Daschle, as it so happens, "serves on the boards of three ethanol companies," according to Larry Rohter of the *New York Times*, "and works at a Washington law firm where, according to his online job description, 'he spends a substantial amount of time providing strategic and policy advice to clients in renewable energy.'"[13] In other words, Daschle is, at least in spirit, an ethanol lobbyist.

Obama knows a few other ethanol lobbyists, too. Soon after he was elected to the U.S. Senate, he drew controversy for flying at subsidized rates on corporate planes, including jets owned by the farming giant Archer Daniels Midland, America's largest ethanol producer.[14] Archer Daniels Midland is being enriched by federal subsidies for which Obama voted.

By supporting the ethanol boondoggle, Obama is putting his own personal interests ahead of the interests of America's energy needs. What's more, he's not doing any favors for the plight of the world's poor and hungry, nor for our environmental health.

A Purdue University study found that biofuels, such as corn ethanol, contribute roughly 60 percent, or $15 billion, to annual food cost increases.[15] "That $15 billion calculates to an additional $130 per household in 2007," according to Ben Lieberman, senior

71

energy policy analyst for The the Heritage Foundation, ""and food prices are considerably higher thus far in 2008."[16]

In fact, since 2005, the price of bread has shot up 37 percent, beef 14 percent, chicken 16 percent, and eggs a whopping 60 percent. And, of course, gas prices have more than doubled.[17] Here, Obama would appear to have the support of the radical animal liberation group, PETA (People for the Ethical Treatment of Animals). PETA, with the support of the United Nations propaganda machine, has embarked on a campaign to convince the public that eating meat causes global warming. The higher the price of meat, the less consumption, and the more successful PETA is in its campaign.

While Americans suffer higher food and gas prices because of Obama's ethanol obsession, elsewhere in the world ethanol production tipped the balance of corn supply and demand, resulting in skyrocketing grain costs and food riots.[18] A *Los Angeles Times* editorial summed it up. "Apparently, no one explained to Congress the basic economic reality that when you dramatically increase the demand for an agricultural product whose supply is limited by the amount of acreage available for farming, prices will rise."[19]

Growing corn for ethanol is extremely land-intensive. It takes one acre of corn to produce roughly 50 gallons of ethanol. Given that Americans consume about 140 billion gallons of gasoline per year, if we were to completely replace our gasoline with corn ethanol, it would require 2.8 billion acres of land. This is more than five times the total actual and potential cropland in the United States.[20]

As excess corn crops swallow more and more farmland to meet Obama's ethanol mandate, it will become much more difficult for pig farmers and cattle and sheep ranchers to stay in business.

Despite ethanol's numerous downsides—billions of tax dollars, high fuel prices, and increased grocery bills—at least we can massage our guilt, believing that ethanol production will save the planet, right? Wrong.

"High prices for corn and other commodities are prompting landowners to remove fallow but ecologically important farmland from a federal conservation program and plant on it instead," the *Los Angeles Times* editorial said. "That increases soil erosion and fertilizer use, contaminating U.S. waterways."[21]

In fact, Princeton University researchers have found that corn ethanol would produce nearly twice the greenhouse gas emissions as regular gasoline over the next three decades.[22] In addition, increased corn ethanol production is contributing to an expanding "dead zone" in the Gulf of Mexico. Nitrogen-based fertilizer from ethanol corn crops is seeping from the fields into the Mississippi River, which carries and deposits the fertilizer into the Gulf, creating a massive, oxygen-depleted area that suffocates sea life.[23]

According to the *Los Angeles Times*:

> Successive energy bills have imposed ever-increasing mandates for blending ethanol (which in the United States is made mostly from corn) with motor fuels. Apparently, no one explained to Congress the basic economic reality that when you dramatically increase the demand for an agricultural product whose supply is limited by the amount of acreage available for farming, prices will rise....
>
> High prices for corn and other commodities are prompting landowners to remove fallow but ecologically important farmland from a federal conservation program and plant on it instead. That increases soil erosion and fertilizer use, contaminating U.S. waterways. Meanwhile, high food prices are boosting inflation....
>
> Tinkering with energy regulation can have disastrous consequences, especially when it's done on behalf of special interests rather than the national interest. Given the number of phenomenally bad proposals for lowering oil prices floating around the Capitol, this lesson could not come at a more critical time.[24]

Barack Obama's close ties to the ethanol industry are not just poisonous for America, but also for the global environment and world hunger. And his plan to subsidize ethanol production will only enrich oil companies, ethanol speculators, and Washington insiders like his friend, Tom Daschle.

NO NUCLEAR, NO COAL, NO OIL SHALE

In 1973, the European energy crisis and "oil shock" hit France. The French, not exactly known for their competitiveness, nonetheless had the wherewithal to begin building nuclear reactors. Today, nearly 80 percent of France's electricity comes from fifty-eight nuclear power plants.[25] The French have found nuclear energy to be safe, clean, reliable—and a good source of income from energy exportation to neighboring countries. Further twisting the knife for Americans, the French nuclear program is founded on American discoveries and American technology.

America, on the other hand, derives just 20 percent of its electricity from nuclear power.[26] We have not built a new reactor in nearly three decades.[27] And while nuclear energy may be a bogeyman to Barack Obama and the anti-energy environmental crowd, most other Americans are now hungry for the plentiful energy that nuclear power can provide.

According to a June 8, 2008, Zogby International Poll, 67 percent of Americans want nuclear power, and only 23 percent (including Barack Obama) do not. Despite this growing demand for nuclear energy, Obama and his elitist friends in the environmental movement remain unmoved.

Even today when plans are proposaled to build forty-five new nuclear reactors by 2030 to help quench America's energy thirst, Obama scoffes at the idea, saying, "It doesn't make sense for America."[28] If we had one hundred new nuclear reactors, we could supply America with enough energy to fulfill the needs of our population growth that will come in the next twenty-five years, an estimated 60 million new consumers, and still have enough left over to export.

So what *does* make sense to Obama? He wants to mandate that the U.S. derive 25 percent of its energy from so-called "sustainable energy sources"—like wind and solar—by 2025,[29] despite the fact that these technologies are unproven, unreliable, and currently comprise less than one percent of America's total energy consumption.[30] His plan calls for siphoning 150 billion taxpayer dollars over the next ten years to fund speculators in the renewable energy lobby who will supposedly turn this pipe dream into a reality.[31] Although it may work sometime in the distant future, such a scheme gambles Americans' precious tax dollars on risky energy speculation. In this endeavor, Obama is reviving a failed Jimmy Carter-era policy—and putting it on steroids.

In 1977, President Jimmy Carter created the Department of Energy and proclaimed solar and wind power the way of the future. Since then, the agency has created over 116,000 federal and government contract jobs,[32] and spent billions of dollars on conservation and renewable energy research.[33] The payoff for this $30 billion dollar, taxpayer-funded joy ride? Less than one percent of America's energy supply. Now Barack Obama wants to throw more of our precious dollars into the wind and solar speculators' black hole.

Obama and his anti-energy friends want to scuttle another proven energy resource: coal. In his official energy platform, Obama threatens to "ban new traditional coal facilities."[34] During his brief stint in the U.S. Senate, he made good on this promise, despite trying to appear to be a friend of coal power—especially during the primary campaign. American consumers and coal miners, especially those in Pennsylvania and West Virginia, should not be deceived.

Coal is extremely important to America's energy supply. Our nation's most abundant resource, coal currently provides over 50 percent of America's total electricity generation—more than twice as much as the next highest energy source (nuclear).[35]

With more coal than any other country in the world, America has more than 250 billion tons, the equivalent of 800 billion barrels of oil and more than three times the amount of Saudi Arabia's oil reserves.[36] Coal presents a virtually unlimited source of energy, so much energy that the U.S. could export—and sell—our surplus supply. In addition, coal power is a whopping 70 percent cleaner than it was thirty years ago.[37] Still, Obama does not see the enormous potential for American coal.

In 2005, shortly after arriving in the Senate, Obama cast the deciding vote in the Senate Environment and Public Works Committee to kill the administration's "Clear Skies" initiative. This measure would have provided much-needed regulatory certainty to coal-fired power plant operators—the same folks whom Obama claimed to support on the campaign trail.[38] It also would have hampered the ability of the environmental movement's legal sharks to file frivolous lawsuits against coal plants.

In 2007, Obama again sided with the environmental lobby to kill a coal-to-liquid incentives bill. Most incredibly, he helped kill this legislation even *after* he had helped craft it *and* publicly supported it.[39] And he ignores the tremendous potential of liquid coal at America's peril.

Coal energy is not a risky, unproven technology. Developed in the early twentieth century, coal liquefaction technology has been utilized ever since. For example, 30 percent of South Africa's oil demand is presently met by liquid coal,[40] an environmentally friendly and clean burning fuel.[41]

In America, we have 600 coal-fired power plants that provide us with 50 percent of our total electricity needs. If we reallocated some of the $150 billion Obama wants to spend on unproven alternative energy sources and invested in building 600 more coal-fired power plants, we would have enough energy for America's future needs *and* we would be a net exporter of energy—like Saudi Arabia.

Unfortunately, proven and inexpensive energy resources are are too dirty for Obama and his fellow environmentalists. While Obama complains that oil exploration would not solve our immediate problem, he's more than happy to promote iffy alternative energy schemes to help America in 2040—our immediate problems be damned.

Apparently, Barack Obama is also opposed to another home-grown energy resource that has the potential to dramatically improve America's security: oil shale.

A study by the Rand Corporation found that an estimated 800 billion barrels of oil—again, more than *three* times Saudi Arabia's total oil reserves—can be found in the oil shale embedded in rock in the corner where Utah borders Colorado and Wyoming.[42] According to Dr. Daniel Fine of MIT, if we begin full- scale production of oil shale within five years, we can completely end our dependence on OPEC oil by 2020.

Yet, in early 2008, rather than permit America to develop this energy gold mine and mitigate our dependence on Middle Eastern oil, Obama voted to lock up access to oil shale.[43]

But this is based on real, proven technology, and yet Barack Obama's elaborate energy plan does not even mention "oil shale"—not once.[44] Why not? Because oil shale would not enrich Obama's supporters in the alternative energy speculation game.

Consider how much American energy Obama would leave untapped:

Proven Oil Reserves in Various Countries v.s. Untapped and Proven Reserves in the United States

Iran: 136 Billion Barrels	ANWR Oil: 19 Billion Barrels
Saudi Arabia: 260 Billion Barrels	Coal: 800 Billion Barrels (BOE*)
Iraq: 115 Billion Barrels	Oil Shale: 800 Billion Barrels (CO, UT, WY)
Venezuela: 80 Billion Barrel	OCS Oil: 86 Billion Barrels
Russia: 60 Billion Barrels	OCS Natural Gas: 70 Billion Barrels (BOE*)
Libya: 41 Billion Barrels	Oil in Production: 21 Billion Barrels
Nigeria: 36 Billion Barrels	Nat. Gas in Prod.: 35 Billion Barrels (BOE*)
Kuwait: 101 Billion Barrels	
UAE: 98 Billion Barrels	
Mexico: 12 Billion Barrels	
Canada: 12 Billion Barrels	

TOTAL: 951 Billion Barrels   U.S. TOTAL: 1.83 Trillion Barrels

*BOE is the barrels of oil equivalent.

The United States does not have an energy crisis. Rather, it has an *environmentalist energy policy crisis*. Obama and environmentalists claim that leaving all of this energy in the ground, and pursuing "clean, renewable energy," will improve human health. But they fail to acknowledge that life expectancy at birth in the U.S. has improved by 66 percent over the last century (forty-seven years in 1900 versus seventy-eight years today).[45] In 1935, when the Social Security Act became law, life expectancy was only 61.7 years.[46] We are living longer, healthier lives today. Why? *Because* of the medical and technological advancements fueled by fossil fuel energy, *not in spite of them*. Had Obama been calling the shots in the last century, we we would no doubt be living in a veritable Dark Ages—and not living very long at that.

OBAMA'S JIMMY CARTER IMPERSONATION

Obama's energy plan for America is simple: Learn to do without.

This is nearly identical to the failed plan that President Jimmy Carter outlined in his infamous "malaise" speech in 1979, when America faced an energy crisis. In his speech, Carter said:

> I'm asking you for your good and for your nation's security to take no unnecessary trips, to use carpools or public transportation whenever you can, to park your car one extra day per week, to obey the speed limit, and to set your thermostats to save fuel. Every act of energy conservation like this is more than just common sense—I tell you it is an act of patriotism.[47]

This widely ridiculed speech is considered the hallmark of the failed Carter presidency. Curiously, Obama seems intent on making it the hallmark of his candidacy. Compare Carter's words with these from Barack Obama nearly thirty years later:

> We can't drive our SUVs and, you know, eat as much as we want and keep our homes on, you know, 72 degrees all the time, whether we're living in the desert or we're living in the tundra, and then just expect every other country is going to say OK.[48]

That is not an energy plan. There is nothing patriotic about going hungry, giving up your car, freezing in the winter, and baking in the summer, just because elitists like Obama want to search for cleaner, more expensive alternatives while they ban access to proven energy reserves for "your own good."

Borrowing from another failed Carter energy plan, Barack Obama also wants to impose a so-called "windfall profits tax" on oil producers. Perhaps Obama is too young to remember those policy failures, but bringing those policies back will doom America to oil and gas shortages, just as they did in the past. As Dr. David Kreutzer, a senior policy analyst at the Heritage Foundation, explains:

> "Excess profits." That's what oil companies are earning, Barack Obama says.... Recent earnings reports from these companies

have set off such a wave of anti-profit proposals that it seems our politicians are reading Mao's *Little Red Book....*

In the popular profits-cause-high-prices theory of economics, there are no risks, and petroleum reserves magically find their way into corporate portfolios. In this world, profits can be confiscated—ahem, taxed—with no adverse effect because profits serve only to inflate costs.

In the real world, the firms that bought, developed and held on to petroleum reserves when petroleum prices were low employed better foresight than those firms that did not. They also put their wealth at risk....

[T]argeting the return on any investment necessarily cuts the incentive to continue making that investment. So, a "windfall" profits tax now will lead to less exploration, less drilling and less oil in the future. When we swing the sledgehammer at oil company profits, we hit future heating oil and gasoline consumers.[49]

No matter. Obama believes a profit tax on oil companies' profits is the right way to reward stockholders who risked their savings and invested their hard-earned money to develop the energy resources on which America depends. Rather than encourage investment, open up ANWR and the OCS, and invest in oil shale, Obama would punish the founders of the feast and bank on the speculation that alternate energy sources will materialize sometime in the distant future.

Obama's windfall profits tax scheme would add a 20 percent tax on the cost of a barrel of oil above $80.[50] The inevitable result will be oil shortages, sky-high gas prices, and economic suicide. Which, apparently, is okay with Obama, even if it is not okay with you as you suffer at the pump.

In June 2008, Obama was asked if he thought high gas prices were good for Americans. "I think that I would have preferred a gradual adjustment," Obama responded."[51]

Most Americans would have preferred no upward adjustment, no energy cost inflation. Barack Obama and the environmental lobbyists with whom he hobnobs don't seem to connect these prices to real families struggling to keep up with rising gas prices. They don't seem to care about workers losing jobs and small businesses failing because of high energy bills. And they don't seem to see the connection with the fact that we are at war with Muslim extremists while we are crushingly dependent on imported oil from Iran, Venezuela, Russia, Saudi Arabia, and Iraq. No, Obama and his green brethren see ignorant masses of fast-driving consumers who should either learn to do without—or take the bus.

In June 2007, Barack Obama voted in favor of a $32 billion tax on oil producers.[52] This tax would have raised the cost of gasoline an estimated $3.26 per gallon over eight years—unnecessarily.[53] Under an Obama regime, Americans would soon long for the good old days when gas was only $4.50 per gallon.

While America is crying out for workable energy solutions, Obama marches in lockstep with energy speculators, regurgitates Jimmy Carter's failed policies, and kowtows to environmental lobbyists and their voting bloc. His so-called energy plan, which is really an energy dependence plan, will accomplish his goal of redistributing American wealth, while we write billion-dollar checks to oil barons in Iran, Venezuela, Russia, and Saudi Arabia. Before long, we will be begging Cuba and China to sell us the oil and gas they harvested just off *our* coast. If Obama is elected president, gas prices will gradually reach the $7.00 and $8.00 range, and, like Jimmy Carter, Obama will lecture America about learning to sacrifice.

As Vaclav Klaus, president of the Czech Republic, has said:

> The largest threat to freedom, democracy, the market economy, and prosperity at the end of the 20th and at the beginning of the 21st century is no longer socialism. It is, instead, the ambitious, arrogant, unscrupulous ideology of environmentalism.[54]

Barack Obama's soaring rhetoric will be replaced by a reality we do not want to face—an energy plan for the road to nowhere. Here's his roadmap:

OBAMA'S TOP TEN ENERGY HITS

1) Obama "strongly reject(s) drilling in the Arctic National Wildlife Refuge (ANWR)."

2) Obama opposes drilling for oil and natural gas in the Outer Continental Shelf (OCS) and believes we should keep all federal moratoriums in place for offshore exploration. China, however, in cooperation with Cuba, aims to drill for oil just miles off the South Florida coast.

3) Calling for a return to the failed Carter-era windfall profits tax—a 20 percent tax on the cost of a barrel of oil above $80—Obama demonstrates a stunning lack of understanding about the commodities markets and other global factors that dictate the price of oil. Anyone who remembers or studies the Carter administration (which must not include Obama) knows that his windfall profits tax had no useful results, hindered domestic energy exploration, and increased our dependence on foreign oil.

4) Obama completely ignores nuclear energy, which provides 20 percent of our nation's electricity and is a zero-emission energy source. While China, Russia, and India look to increase the role of nuclear power in their energy portfolios, and nuclear plants currently power 80 percent of France's electricity, Obama dismisses the important

role nuclear power could play in achieving America's energy self-sufficiency.

5) Obama says he would consider implementing standards that would ban new traditional coal facilities despite the abundance of coal energy resources. (The U.S. accounts for 27 percent of the world's coal supply—the equivalent of about 800 billion barrels of oil and more than three times Saudi Arabia's oil reserves). Under Obama's plan, this rich resource could go untapped as America strives for energy independence and brings other technologies to bear.

6) In 2007, Obama voted for the renewable fuels bill that further increased the ethanol mandate. Now recognized as a failed policy, this legislation caused farmers to divert corn crops from food to fuel use, increasing food costs by $130 per family per year.

7) Obama's energy plan increases the government's role in fostering the development of technologies to reduce emissions and alternatives to fossil fuels while shunning other proven energy sources such as nuclear power and traditional coal.

8) Obama's energy plan would require the United States to get at least 25 percent of its electricity from renewable sources such as wind, solar and geothermal energy by 2025. Given that these energy sources currently account for less than 1 percent of U.S. electricity supply, his goal is unrealistic.

9) Obama supports raising CAFE standards, which: damage the already reeling American auto industry; make vehicles significantly more expensive; and make vehicles significantly less crash-worthy, resulting in thousands of additional highway deaths per year.

10) The fact is, in Obama's America, we would be more dependent on oil producers in the Middle East, and continue to fall victim to the prices they set for American consumers.

For new, breaking information on Barack Obama since this book was published, please go to www.audacityofdeceit.com. If you have friends who would like to receive this chapter, or any of the chapters in this book, please refer them to the same Web site where they can download the chapter of their choice for free.

CHAPTER SEVEN

FREE TRADE, FREE PEOPLE

"[P]rotectionism is being used by some American politicians as a cheap form of nationalism, a fig leaf for those unwilling to maintain America's military strength and who lack the resolve to stand up to real enemies — countries that would use violence against us or our allies. Our peaceful trading partners are not our enemies; they are our allies. We should beware of the demagogues who are ready to declare a trade war against our friends — weakening our economy, our national security, and the entire free world — all while cynically waving the American flag. The expansion of the international economy is not a foreign invasion; it is an American triumph, one we worked hard to achieve, and something central to our vision of a peaceful and prosperous world of freedom."[1]

—President Ronald Reagan

YOU CAN HARDLY BLAME American voters if they are befuddled and bewildered (or flat-out bored) when it comes to the issue of trade. Talk of "globalization" — which can be defined in countless ways depending on who is talking — free trade, tariffs, subsidies, NAFTA, CAFTA, GATT, or the WTO is hardly the stuff of exciting dinner table conversation, and it's hard to separate fact from spin.

Nonetheless, the trade issue is of growing importance in the 2008 elections. When a presidential candidate like Obama proposes to renege on a bipartisan deal affecting world trade, Americans really should sit up and take notice.[2]

As Kimberly Strassel notes in the *Wall Street Journal*, Obama's "primary victory marked the end of many things, and one looks to be his party's twenty-year experiment with ideological centrism...the intellectual soul of the Democratic Party is now firmly left."[3]

Strassel continues by saying that the "New Democrats"— led by Bill Clinton—were born in response to Ronald Reagan's triumphs, and they preached, among other things, an economic centrism.[4] "Party liberals despised Mr. Clinton's embrace of free trade," she writes, "but no one could deny his success at giving the party its first two full terms in the White House since FDR. So they shut up and went along."[5]

OBAMA GETS "BIG LABOR" ENDORSEMENT

Trade has always been used as a way to wage war, albeit an economic war.

During the presidential primary, Barack Obama's populist rhetoric denounced Bill Clinton, Hillary Clinton, and big business for destroying U.S. jobs and shifting them overseas as a result of free trade agreements.

In doing so, Obama not only destroyed Hillary Clinton but also the positive, if not great, economic trade message of the Clinton presidency.

The very fact that organized labor is shifting its focus from corporate America to international trade agreements is testament that labor has an even bigger enemy today—foreign competition. In taking on this new enemy, labor is also donning its protectionist armor by demanding that new trade agreements incorporate onerous labor and environmental standards.

The so-called "Blue Green Alliance" links America's 15.4 million labor union members with Americans who are part of the international environmentalist movement. This partnership made for an unbeatable combination that Obama used to secure his primary victory.

A prime example is the Sierra Club's support for Barack Obama. They supported Obama's attacks on NAFTA, because they wanted to be a player in the trade agreement process, at the highest levels of negotiation, in order to push their environmental agenda on the rest of the world. Without the clout of the trade agreement, environmental groups would have to negotiate directly with foreign countries, who would only laugh at their superior pretensions. "We were one of the groups that opposed NAFTA," said Margrete Strand, the Sierra Club's trade expert, "because we felt there had to be a binding environmental chapter" in the agreement.[6] In other words, the Sierra Club opposed NAFTA because they weren't included in telling other countries what they should do.

On the other side of the table, rather than advancing labor's interest in the era of globalization and free trade, the AFL-CIO joined forces with the extreme environmental movement in an effort to saddle trade agreements with unpalatable environmental and labor provisos.

Narrowly and selfishly focused, these two groups fail to see the benefit of cheap goods for retired Americans or those living on fixed incomes. They refuse to accept the inevitable— that expanding trade is vital to growing America's economy and labor market. Even Al From, founder of the Democratic Leadership Council, accepts this premise:

> [I]f Democrats are serious about turning the economy around, we have to be willing to tell people that job and income growth depends on Washington's willingness to get its fiscal house in order, invest in people and technology, and, yes, expand trade.
>
> History proves that expanding trade and productivity help create growth. We learned that the hard way when the Smoot-Hawley Tariff Act of the Hoover administration helped crush trade and exacerbate the Great Depression. Conversely, we have seen trade drive the economy during the great expansions of the 1960s [Johnson] and the 1990's [Clinton].
>
> Today with the economy in or near recession, the market-opening agreements of the 1990's are proving their value. Even while domestic finance, real estate, and consumer sectors have begun to contract, manufacturing exports have jumped by $200 billion since 2005. Meanwhile services sector and

agricultural trade surpluses have soared so that along with government spending, exports to places like Europe, Brazil, and China are proving to be the only spark keeping us out of a full fledged slowdown.[7]

Seventy-eight years after the Smoot-Hawley Tariff Act, politics is once again defeating common sense. As columnist John Fund observes:

> There was another period when raw politics was allowed to trump what many in Congress privately admitted was common sense. In the spring of 1930, as the economic downturn set off by the previous year's stock market crash set in, Congress was debating the Smoot-Hawley tariff bill that sought to raise U.S. import barriers to record levels.
>
> Most of the leading economists of the day opposed Smoot-Hawley. A front-page *New York Times* headline on May 5, 1930, read: "1,028 Economists Ask Hoover to Veto Pending Tariff Bill." But for entirely selfish and shortsighted reasons, both Congress and President Hoover went along with the protectionist hysteria. As a result, the Great Depression was probably deepened and extended for years.[8]

Obama's trade war would take on the failed protectionist policies of the Hoover administration in an effort to win over organized labor and destroy the Bill and Hillary Clinton legacy. The outcome for Hoover and America was nothing short of a disaster. For Obama, the immediate outcome may well be the presidency, but storm clouds are forming on America's long-term economic horizon.

Reagan and Clinton convinced the world to invest hundreds of billions of dollars in the American economy, because they believed in its ability to create products and open markets. The largest economy in the world for over one hundred years, we have commanded over 25 percent of the world GNP, and we will do so for the next fifty years, if we have free trade.

Trade, or the lack thereof, has been used as a weapon and as a tool. Prior to World War II, America and Europe used trade barriers to deny Japan access to a variety of materials in an effort to stop them from joining forces with Germany and building up their war machine. On the other hand, today, America heavily relies on trade with friends and foes alike. For example, we import a variety of vital minerals that are completely or nearly non-existent in the United States. These include arsenic, tin, and manganese, and twenty to forty others. Without these vital minerals, a number of products would be seriously affected, factories would close, and jobs would be lost. Without free trade, we would be without metals that we need to make pesticides, wood preservatives, heat and acoustic installation, fire proofing, electronic devices, glass coating, fertilizer, nuclear fuel, TVs, microwaves, auto parts, jet engines, cement superconductors, pressure gauges, medical supplies, medical equipment, optical lenses, alloys for aerospace industry, solar cells, electronics, pharmaceuticals, jet engines, air planes, and a long list of other products. This list indicates that we might face serious and unintended consequences if Obama, the labor unions, and the environmentalists engage the U.S. in a trade war.

JOB CREATION

The trade agreements initiated by Clinton and Reagan opened up markets around the world, and in the process, helped developing democratic countries lock in and implement economic and political reforms effectively, spur regional integration and enhance the prospects for investment and economic growth. Those trade agreements were also a boon to America's economy.

American exports today are booming—up 50 percent in three years. The U.S. in 2007 was the world's largest exporter with $1.3 trillion in exports, or about 20 percent of our Gross Domestic Product and, by inference, 20 percent of the nation's jobs.[9] Obama will stop this growth unless he can satisfy labor and environmental interests.

Obama tells us that 900,000 jobs were lost to NAFTA, but one study showed exports of goods support 6 million American jobs, exports of services support 5 million jobs, and foreign companies moving to the U.S. to be close to consumers employ another 5 million American workers. That's 16 million American jobs that would be affected by Obama's arrogant trade policies.

Today, U.S. annual incomes are $1 trillion higher, or $9,000 higher per household, due to increased trade liberalization since 1945.[10] And if the world's remaining trade barriers were completely eliminated, U.S. incomes could increase by an additional $500 billion, adding roughly $4,500 per household.[11]

President Clinton and President Reagan wanted to create jobs by opening markets. Both believed Communist countries such as China, Russia, and Vietnam could only compete by adopting free enterprise and free market economies. And they believed other countries would have to adopt America's free trade strategies.

Presidents Clinton and Reagan believed that with free trade, Americans could pour hundreds of billions of dollars into the American economy, because the world believed America could create products, develop technology, and control a growing share of international markets, and America did. Now Obama's rhetoric fueled by his hysterical non-governmental partners could have the opposite effect. Here's a look at what free trade agreements have meant for the U.S. since the Carter administration ended in 1981:[12]

American Exports Have Increased U.S. Export Totals (in $ USD)			
	End Reagan Era 1989	End Clinton Era 2000	Today 2007
Canada	$78.3 billion	$176.4 billion	$248.4 billion
China	$5.8 billion	$16.3 billion	$65.2 billion
Mexico	$25.0 billion	$111.7 billion	$136.5 billion
Vietnam	$10.5 million	$376.0 million	$1.9 billion
Russia	$0	$2.3 billion	$7.4 billion
Brazil	$4.8 billion	$15.4 billion	$24.6 billion
India	$2.5 billion	$3.6 billion	$17.6 billion

Obama, labor unions, and the environmentalists also neglect to mention that people on fixed incomes and low salaries are the chief beneficiaries of free trade. Free trade with poorer countries improves the buying power of middle and lower income consumers. Wealthier consumers seldom shop at Wal-Mart, Target, Sears, and other discount stores where much of the merchandise is manufactured inexpensively and imported to the U.S. from such countries as China, Vietnam, and Mexico.

As a result of free trade agreements, the inflation rate for low-income Americans is six points lower than that for the wealthiest Americans.[13] Labor and environmental lobbyists ignore this fact because their salaries would place them among America's wealthiest.

Despite an army of statistics that demonstrates the benefits of free trade, Obama, organized labor, and environmentalists continue to argue that their primary concern is raising the wages of foreign labor and argue, incorrectly, that low wages abroad translate into lost jobs at home. That notion is a tough sell, however, as Fareed Zakaria points out in a recent *Newsweek* article:

> There are no serious economists or experts who believe that low wages in Mexico or China or India is the fundamental reason that American factories close down. And labor and environmental standards would do little to change the reality of high wage differentials between poor and rich countries' workers.[14]

In fact, free trade has made America the economic paradigm for most of the past century. The U.S. has 5 percent of the world's population, but we control 25 percent of the world's wealth. American innovators have never been frightened of risking time, money, and jobs to increase that number. We love to compete, but competition has some inherent trade-offs. Some jobs might be lost in pursuit of open markets, but, in the long-run, America ends up gaining far more from free trade than it loses—especially where jobs are concerned. The notion of America as a free trade winner is echoed by Chris Farrell in *BusinessWeek*:

> The case for freer trade and open markets is overwhelming. Economic evidence and economic history alike support the view that freer trade over time invigorates economic growth by encouraging the spread of new commercial ideas, new technologies, and new ways of organizing everyday life. Consumers enjoy lower prices and greater choice. Competition from overseas rivals encourages corporate efficiency and innovation.[15]

DEMOCRATS' ANTI-TRADE DYNAMIC

Rather than encourage international environmentalists to enter direct talks with China—the biggest polluter in the world today—Obama intends to talk for those groups and force China to accept their demands, even if it results in higher prices at Wal-Mart or requires American tax dollars to help clean up pollution worldwide.

Obama intends to campaign for better working conditions and higher wages for Chinese workers. He is still that community activist that never had a job in the free enterprise system. Only now he wants to be president so he can be an international community activist. During a February 2008 visit to a GM plant in Janesville, Wisconsin, Obama vowed that he will "end tax breaks for companies who ship jobs overseas and give breaks to companies who create good jobs with decent wages here in America."[16]

Obama fails to recognize that free trade agreements are not much of an agreement if only one country stands to principally benefit. Our trading partners have no interest in becoming America's lackey and only want an agreement that benefits *all* parties to the agreement.

The marriage of organized labor and environmentalists comes as no surprise. This "Blue Green" Alliance, as the AFL-CIO calls it, is nothing more than a potent poison pill for would-be trade agreements. When it comes to their objections to free trade, environmentalists are on even shakier footing than labor interests, since the thrust of their argument is predicated upon the global warming sham. Illustrating this point, *National Review's* Rich Lowry writes:

> The world has been warming since 1998, and an article in the journal *Nature* says warming won't pick up again until 2015. Since global warming is a long term trend, a decade long or more stall in temperatures doesn't mean much—except that environmentalists have banked so much politically on whipping up hysteria based on imminent catastrophe.[17]

All America can hope for is that, by the time his re-election comes around in 2012, Obama will deny ever having cavorted with the global-warming crowd.

China has created a huge new market of consumers, moving almost 500 million people out of poverty. At the beginning of Reagan's presidency in 1981, one billion people were engaged in the world of trade. Today, that number has doubled to 2 billion. In twenty-five years it will be 4 billion. These are America's new customers for products and services. We *must* continue the

Clinton-Reagan policy of capturing these global markets, not paralyzing them with pointless trade restrictions.

CUSTOMERS NEEDED FOR AMERICAN PRODUCTS

America needs new customers for our products and services. As Baby Boomers begin to exit the labor market and immigration controls limit new immigrants to only 1.2 million entering the country per year, America will grow by 65 million people in the next twenty years. At the same time, Europe will have no population growth. Clearly America will have to forge new customers and trading partners to support its factories and create a market for its manufacturing products, technology, and services.

Consider the example of air conditioning in China. According to Dr. Simon Wang, "In a society like China experiencing a capitalist boom, consumers are treating themselves to luxuries that were previously unavailable. Air conditioning is one of them." The number of households owning air conditioning units has tripled in China in the past decade, and more than 20 million units are now sold there each year.[18]

As the wealth of our trading partners grows, so do the demands for American goods. Foreign customers now want medicines, high tech products, appliances, and better clothes.

India's economic growth will catch up to Britain's in twelve years, with the nation promising to become the world's third-largest trading partner within forty years.

The shift in the location of top multi-national companies from places like the United States and Europe to Asia, South America, and Africa underscores the importance of future free trade agreements, which will enrich the workforce in their countries and create demand for American products.

Combined, China and India have almost ten times the population of the U.S. In order to grow their economies, both of these countries will continue the road to free markets, creating consumers who want better products, many of which are made in America.

Companies like Wal-Mart will benefit from the supply of goods from China and other countries. America's consumers will benefit from the resulting lower prices at stores like Wal-Mart, and China's population will realize the Western dream of more wealth with better medicines, for example, and better technology than ever before.

OBAMA'S FREE TRADE FREEZE

New trading partners are important as these economies expand the need for America's agricultural products. In the last fifteen years, American agricultural products grew by 65 percent. The growth in product sales in Canada and Mexico, our two NAFTA partners, was 156 percent, almost three times faster than the rest of the world. Today, Mexico is a democracy with an economically sound and stable government, a robust economy, and more job creation than it experienced in the pre-NAFTA years.

Rather than letting free trade and free markets lift the world's poor out of poverty, Obama sponsored the "Global Poverty Act" (S. 2433) in the U.S. Senate. This bill would allocate seven-tenths of a percent of America's gross national product to be spent on foreign aid, trade, and debt relief. For the record, seven-tenths of a percent of the GNP amounts to a whopping $845 *billion*! That means millions of dollars for the farmer in Kenya, the coffee bean grower in Columbia, and other poor living in countries like Korea and Peru—with nothing in return for American companies or consumers.

Obama's foreign aid bill is yet another attempt at the redistribution of wealth on a global scale. It would create jobs, but only five percent of them would be American jobs. We would simply hand over our tax dollars to the United Nations, which would distribute the money, and Obama, in the process, will keep his commitment to use *our* money "to heal the world." As if the fathomless gifts of charity, democracy, medical and other technologies, and hope that generous and industrious Americans export to the world—asking nothing in return—somehow aren't enough.

The Global Poverty Act begs an interesting question: How is it okay for Obama to propose that American taxpayers foot the bill for the Global Poverty Act, which creates foreign jobs and imposes excessive environmental regulations, while he sides with organized labor over the loss of American jobs to free trade agreements? It seems like Obama really has his priorities backward.

Obama fails to understand that everyone benefits from free trade, and we can only negotiate from strength with a president who will be firm in negotiations, not someone who must seek approval from partners who gave him money and votes to win the Democratic presidential nomination and the general election in November.

Do we really need a president like Obama intent on creating a highly regulated economy, with trade barriers up, closing markets, and a return to Hoover protectionist policies?

As Democratic foreign policy adviser Stuart Gottlieb cautions:

> The message Democrats are sending to the world is clear: You cannot trust America to honor its trade agreements, even with developing nations struggling to enter the global middle class. This is a far cry from Obama's Lincolnesque promise in his Democratic nomination victory speech June 3rd to restore "our image as the last, best hope on earth."[19]

America should be proud that Presidents Reagan and Clinton used globalization, not foreign aid, to reduce poverty and raise living standards around the world. These presidents demonstrated that when we open up markets, trade will increase American wealth by 10 percent per year. When we close markets and tinker with existing trade agreements, major job losses can result. Yes, free trade agreements can cause some job losses, but they will create two new jobs for every one lost. American technology and innovation are the keys to producing products cheaper and capturing more of the international trade America needs in order to grow.

The largest economy in the world for more than one hundred years, the United States will continue its domination as long as free trade continues to be a priority for our nation. If we destroy our free trade legacy, however, by adopting the protectionist agenda of Obama Blue Green Alliance of organized labor and the environmental movement, then we are in for a truly frightening economic period.

For new, breaking information on Barack Obama since this book was published, please go to www.audacityofdeceit.com. If you have friends who would like to receive this chapter, or any of the chapters in this book, please refer them to the same Web site where they can download the chapter of their choice for free.

CHAPTER EIGHT

CHANGING JUSTICE

"But the work of the high court has had vast systemic influence over the lives of all Americans, an effect that lasts through generations. In the tripartite tussle, it's no contest: SCOTUS rules.

"The display of the Ten Commandments in public buildings. The scope of the eminent domain. The reading of rights to defendants. The ability of taxpayers to litigate against faith-based government-funded programs. School prayer. Medical marijuana. Campaign ads. And that's before you get to desegregation, abortion, affirmative action and capital punishment. If you try to register to vote in Indiana and are turned away because you don't have a government-issued photo ID, that's because the Supremes just ruled, 6-3, that that's OK."

— Anna Quindlen, The 2008 Bench Press

W HEN THEY WROTE the U.S. Constitution, our Founding Fathers created three separate but equal branches of government—the legislative branch (Congress), the executive branch (the presidency), and the judicial branch (the federal courts, including the U.S. Supreme Court). The reasons were clear: to prevent any one government entity from wielding too much power and influence. Without checks and balances, a president, the Founders worried, could become like a king, an elected legislature could trample rights, and a judiciary could rule in favor of granting itself more power. The three branches of government exist to keep the whole in check.

Now, more than two hundred years since the earliest Americans threw off the yoke of oppression, a new threat to our freedom is coming from a place few expected—from within the judicial branch, our own court system.

Today, most of our political battles emerge between the presidency and Congress. But when was the last time the executive and legislative branches acted in concert to stop abuses perpetrated by the judicial branch? It is difficult to recall such a time. These days, our presidents and legislators behave as if our federal courts are the sole arbiters of law, justice, and constitutionalism. When the White House and Congress are split between Republican and Democratic control, we often hear complaints about decisions of the federal court, whose rulings have the same weight and effect as law, even though the legislative and executive branches are responsible for passing our laws.

When rendering its decisions, the nation's highest judicial body—the U.S. Supreme Court—has been particularly guilty on many occasions of disregarding not only the will of the people but also the will of our elected officials. The U.S. Constitution is supposed to guide justices' decisions, but too often their opinions are based on political and personal beliefs, not hard-and-fast, clear-cut constitutional principles. Their abysmal decisions are left unchallenged—unchecked, if you will—by the other two branches of government, which are supposed to provide the "check and balance" against a renegade federal court system.

If Barack Obama wins the Oval Office in 2008, he will also likely enjoy a Democratic Congress, perhaps with enough new Democratic senators and Democrat representatives in the House to give him almost veto-proof power. The only branch that will stand between Obama and absolute power will be the judicial branch—the Supreme Court and federal judiciary.

Very quickly, however, Obama will be able to tilt the balance of the federal courts. Democrats, currently refusing to approve judicial nominations until Obama is elected president, will hand the new president the opportunity to appoint forty-nine judges to fill federal vacancies.[1]

It will only be only a matter of time before Obama is able to tip the balance of the Supreme Court, as well. All but two of the nine Supreme Court judges are over seventy, and one justice is in his late eighties. Within his first term, Obama will likely have the opportunity to appoint anyone he wants to the Court, and the Congress will undoubtedly be willing to do his bidding.

How? Presidents select our Supreme Court justices. Based on Obama's record—in word and deed, as a lawyer and legislator—we can conclude that Obama will select justices, not for their regard for our laws, but rather, for their political beliefs. And their beliefs about America won't be anything like those of our Founding Fathers. Traditional American values will become a thing of the past, and worse, they will be enshrined in legal "precedence"—which our president and dutiful minions in Congress will consider untouchable.

Then the Courts, Congress, and President Obama will no longer serve as a check and balance on a runaway power.

If Obama becomes our next president, assuming he wins a second term, he would have an opportunity to appoint one, and perhaps as many as four justices (Justice John Paul Stevens is eighty-eight; Justice Anthony M. Kennedy will be seventy-three by the time of the November election).

Consider what Obama said about Samuel Alito, nominated by President Bush to the high court in October 2005 to replace retiring Associate Justice Sandra Day O'Connor. *Despite* admitting that Alito was imminently qualified to be an associate justice, Obama voted against his nomination anyway, because Alito's decisions were based on constitutional law and precedence, not on Obama's political activist agenda.

"While I certainly believe that Judge Samuel Alito has the training and the qualifications necessary to serve as a Supreme Court Justice, after a careful review of his record, I simply cannot vote for his nomination," Obama said in a statement

THE AUDACITY OF DECEIT

released by his U.S. Senate office. "The Judicial Branch of our government is a place where any American citizen can stand equal before the eyes of the law. Yet, in examining Judge Alito's many decisions, I have seen extraordinarily consistent support for the powerful against the powerless, for the employer against the employee, for the president against the Congress and the Judiciary....By ruling this way so many times over a course of so many years, Judge Alito simply does not inspire confidence that he will serve as an independent voice on the U.S. Supreme Court."[2]

Obama accused Alito—who served, among other posts, as a U.S. attorney and assistant to the U.S. Solicitor General before spending fifteen years as a federal judge for the Third U.S. Court of Appeals—of ruling in a manner supportive of "an overreaching federal government against individual rights and liberties."[3] The truth is, Alito's prior decisions as a federal judge were in line with the best traditions of constitutionalism—precisely the kind of justice that best serves the interests of all three branches of government and the people those branches were established to serve.

First of all, Alito had more federal judicial experience than 105 of the 109 justices had when they were appointed.[4] Secondly—and most importantly—even those who disagreed with him politically said he was a judge who based decisions not on what was politically expedient or popular at the time, or on his personal beliefs, but on what was constitutionally permissible.

Edward Feulner, Ph.D., president of the Heritage Foundation, describes Alito's record and what others who are political opposites of him had to say about his ability to issue constitutional rulings:

> [T]he the most important thing to know about the soft-spoken judge from New Jersey is that he understands the proper role of a judge. His record indicates he won't make law—he'll interpret the laws as written, rather than how he wants them to be. It's also clear he'll remain faithful to the actual meaning of the

Constitution, instead of stretching it to mean whatever he wants it to mean. How can we know that? Because even those who disagree with Alito politically say that's what he'll do. Former federal Judge Timothy K. Lewis is a liberal who has worked with Alito on the Third Circuit. He told the *Los Angeles Times* that Alito "is not result-oriented. He is an honest conservative judge who believes in judicial restraint and judicial deference." Lewis isn't alone in that view. He also related a conversation he had with Judge A. Leon Higginbotham, Jr., a legendary liberal judge in his day. "Sam Alito is my favorite judge to sit with on this court," Higginbotham told Lewis in 1992. "He is a wonderful judge and a terrific human being. Sam Alito is my kind of conservative. He is intellectually honest. He doesn't have an agenda."[5]

Feulner also notes that Kate Pringle, a former law clerk for Alito, told the *Times*, "He was not, in my personal experience, an ideologue. He pays attention to the facts of cases and applies the law in a careful way. He is conservative in that sense. His opinions don't demonstrate an ideological slant." Since she worked for Alito, we might conclude that she is of the same ideology. Not so; she voted for Senator John Kerry for president in 2004.[6]

Alito's qualifications were also top-rated by the American Bar Association, which has a history and reputation of supporting left-wing causes.[7]

Even more telling about his activist nature, Obama also voted against Judge John Roberts, President Bush's choice to serve as Chief Justice of the Supreme Court.

Lauding praise on Roberts, Obama again said, "There is absolutely no doubt in my mind Judge Roberts is qualified to sit on the highest court in the land. Moreover, he seems to have the comportment and the temperament that makes for a good judge. He is humble, he is personally decent, and he appears to be respectful of different points of view. It is absolutely clear to me that Judge Roberts truly loves the law."[8]

And yet, because Roberts did not hold a more activist view of his role as a judge who would be sitting on the highest court in the land, Obama said he couldn't vote to confirm him:

> The problem I face—a problem that has been voiced by some of my other colleagues, both those who are voting for Mr. Roberts and those who are voting against Mr. Roberts—is that while adherence to legal precedent and rules of statutory or constitutional construction will dispose of 95 percent of the cases that come before a court, so that both a Scalia and a Ginsburg will arrive at the same place most of the time on those 95 percent of the cases—what matters on the Supreme Court is those 5 percent of cases that are truly difficult.... The bottom line is this: I will be voting against John Roberts' nomination. I do so with considerable reticence. I hope that I am wrong. I hope that this reticence on my part proves unjustified and that Judge Roberts will show himself to not only be an outstanding legal thinker but also someone who upholds the Court's historic role as a check on the majoritarian impulses of the executive branch and the legislative branch. I hope that he will recognize who the weak are and who the strong are in our society.[9]

Later in his speech, Obama said, "These groups on the right and left should not resort to the sort of broad-brush dogmatic attacks that have hampered the process in the past and constrained each and every senator in this Chamber from making sure that they are voting on the basis of their conscience." And he criticized what he described as the "unyielding, unbending, dogmatic approach to judicial confirmation [that] has in large part been responsible for the kind of poisonous atmosphere that exists in this Chamber regarding judicial nominations." And yet his left-wing activism was "unyielding, unbending" and "dogmatic" in his steadfast refusal to support a pair of Supreme Court nominees he himself said were imminently qualified to be on the bench.

As Obama has proven by his disapproval of Alito and Roberts, knowledge and support of the U.S. Constitution isn't what matters to him. What matters instead is *judicial activism*—whether or not a judge can render decisions based on his or her social and political concerns and beliefs—and the Constitution, the nation's highest law of the land, be damned.

"When the nomination of John Roberts to be chief justice of the Supreme Court came up in the Senate in 2005, Sen. Barack Obama argued that the role of a justice is to favor the 'weak' over the 'strong,'" writes Terrence P. Jeffrey, the editor-in-chief of *Cybercast News Service.* "When the nomination of Sam Alito came up in January 2006, he made the same argument. Obama does not want a Supreme Court that preserves the rule of law, he wants a Supreme Court that wages class war under color of law."[10]

Who does he believe consists of the "weak?" Who is "strong?" Which group deserves to win the "hearts" of the Supreme Court? Which doesn't? What should be the deciding factors?

Rather than probe the inner feelings of John Roberts—who admitted that it is difficult for him to talk about his personal feelings and values because that's not how he was trained—Obama should have listened more carefully to the future chief justice's Senate Judiciary Committee testimony, in which he said:

> Judges are like umpires. Umpires don't make the rules; they apply them. I will decide every case based on the record, according to the rule of law, without fear or favor, to the best of my ability. And I will remember that it's my job to call balls and strikes, and not to pitch or bat.[11]

In May 2008, the California Supreme Court overturned that state's ban on gay marriages, saying, in part, sexual orientation, like race or gender, "does not constitute a legitimate basis upon which to deny or withhold legal rights."[12] Obama, for his part, said he opposes same-sex marriages but supports civil unions—which is the same thing as supporting the concept behind the idea—gay unions—minus the formality of marriage, because he feels it is a civil rights matter, not a legal issue. So his approval of the lifestyle means he is likely to appoint U.S. justices to the nation's highest court who *also* approve—which means that, despite the fact that most states and the federal government currently prohibit gay marriage, that could be the law of the land someday in the near future.

No More Detentions!

Above all else, Barack Obama cannot be allowed to be in a position to influence the nation's highest court because his experience in foreign affairs would ultimately put every American man, woman, and child at risk.

In June 2008 the U.S. Supreme Court—in a ruling against America's handling of suspected terrorists—said the then-270 suspects being held at the Guantanamo Bay, Cuba, detention facility had a right to challenge their detention in U.S. courts.

Remember that these are *enemy combatants*, they're not citizens, and they've now been granted rights under the Constitution of the United States.

Barack Obama, however, agreed with the decision.

"What we know is that, in previous terrorist attacks—for example, the first attack against the World Trade Center—we were able to arrest those responsible, put them on trial. They are currently in U.S. prisons, incapacitated," he said in an interview with ABC News. "And the fact that the administration has not tried to do that has created a situation where not only have we never actually put many of these folks on trial, but we have destroyed our credibility when it comes to rule of law all around the world, and given a huge boost to terrorist recruitment in countries that say, 'Look, this is how the United States treats Muslims....'"[13]

Other officials who have practical, hands-on experience in dealing with terrorists and are not posing for special interest groups, are much more realistic about the threat they pose to the nation. Former CIA Director James Woolsey says Obama has "an extremely dangerous and extremely naive approach toward terrorism...and toward dealing with prisoners captured overseas who have been engaged in terrorist attacks against the United States."[14]

And, seven years after the 9/11 attacks, Al Qaeda *still* remains the biggest terrorist threat to the United States, according to the U.S. State Department. Al Qaeda "utilizes terrorism, as well as subversion, propaganda, and open warfare; it seeks weapons of mass destruction in order to inflict the maximum possible damage on anyone who stands in its way, including other Muslims and/or elders, women and children," says the department, in its annual report released in April 2008.[15]

Yet, in Obama's America, one of the terrorists' best weapons could be our own Supreme Court.

Further, the Supreme Court's decision that the Constitution guarantees individuals the right to keep handguns in the home—a big victory for gun owners—could be overturned if Obama is president. The *Wall Street Journal* provided a glimpse of what could lie ahead in an Obama presidency:

> Justice Breyer, who wrote a companion dissent, takes a more devious tack. He wants to establish an "interest-balancing test" to weigh the Constitutionality of particular restrictions on gun ownership. This balancing test is best understood as a roadmap for vitiating the practical effects of *Heller* going forward.
>
> Using Justice Breyer's "test," judges could accept the existence of an individual right to bear arms in theory, while whittling it down to nothing by weighing that right against the interests of the government in preventing gun-related violence. Having set forth this supposedly neutral standard, Justice Breyer shows his policy hand by arguing that under this standard the interests of the District of Columbia would outweigh Mr. Heller's interest in defending himself, and the ban should thus be upheld.[16]

Justice Breyer's opinion on the *Heller* case is important, since one of the few seemingly clear statements Obama has made on the courts is that the next judge will be a clone of Stephen Breyer:[17] A judge who would work to empower the government and restrict individual liberty. A judge who would protect gay rights, abortion rights, and the rights of criminals to rape children without having to face the death penalty.[18] A judge who would join Breyer and three other justices on the Supreme Court in reversing the Second Amendment rights recently upheld by Americans.

In addition, a liberal could reverse other close decisions if the opportunity presented itself, such as:

- Evidence Gained After Improper Entry Is Still Admissible (June 15, 2006): Court decides, 5-4, in *Hudson v. Michigan,* that even if police fail to "knock and announce" before entering a home to execute a search warrant—as required by the Constitution—evidence obtained in the search may be admitted at trial.

- Court Upholds Kansas's Death Penalty Law (June 26, 2006): Justices, voting 5-4 in *Kansas v. Marsh,* overturn a 2004 Kansas Supreme Court decision that declared the state's death penalty statue is unconstitutional. The U.S. Supreme Court rules that the state law that makes the death penalty automatic if mitigating and aggravating evidence hold equal weight is valid.

- Three-Strikes Law Validated (March 5, 2003): In two separate decisions, the court, 5-4, upholds California's "three strikes and you're out" law that calls for long sentences when a person is convicted of a third offense.

- School Voucher Victory (June 27, 2002): Court, 5-4, upholds use of public funds for tuition at private religious schools under Cleveland voucher program.

- Sex Predator Law Upheld (June 23, 1997): Justices rule, 5-4, that states may confine some offenders to mental hospitals after they have served prison sentences if they are deemed likely to continue crimes.

One name comes to mind that qualifies as the type of person who thinks like Breyer that could be appointed to the Supreme Court in an Obama presidency: Hillary Clinton.

THE BIG PICTURE

Obama's key qualifier for Supreme Court judges appears not to be whether individuals are capable of interpreting the Constitution and applying it to cases. Rather, Obama wants his justices to act on their emotions, feelings, and "empathy."

"We need somebody who's got the heart, the empathy, to recognize what it's like to be a young teenage mom," Obama told a Planned Parenthood conference in Washington, D.C., in 2007. "The empathy to understand what it's like to be poor, or African-American, or gay, or disabled, or old. And that's the criteria by which I'm going to be selecting my judges."[19]

It's quite possible that the most important sleeper issue of this election isn't terrorism, or energy, or the economy. Rather, it is the question of exactly what sort of justices our next president will select for the U.S. Supreme Court. The man who makes those choices will be deciding whether America will continue to be based on the revolutionary model that our forefathers fought for and died to create, or rather become some left-wing, social, cultural, hedonistic experiment that more closely resembles the declining days of the Roman Empire by giving absolute power to Barack Obama.

In other words, will we continue to be the United States of America, or will our nation be transformed into something it was never intended to be: a country ruled by a one-party system controlled by one man hungry for the power to change the world.

For new, breaking information on Barack Obama since this book was published, please go to www.audacityofdeceit.com. If you have friends who would like to receive this chapter, or any of the chapters in this book, please refer them to the same Web site where they can download the chapter of their choice for free.

CHAPTER NINE

CHANGING AMERICAN HEALTHCARE

"Rather than educating us on the issues, American political campaigns are run on themes, images, and messages which are evocative, but content-free sound bytes."[1]

—Bruce Dixon, *BlackAgendaReport.com*, in criticizing Barack Obama's healthcare plan

*I*MAGINE THAT ONE NIGHT you become violently ill, so ill that your spouse must drive you to the hospital emergency room. Eight hours later, you finally see a doctor for the first time. When you complain about the agonizingly long wait, the doctor apologizes, explaining that there were thirty people ahead of you, most of whom were non-English speaking, illegal aliens who were all eligible for taxpayer-funded healthcare under Barack Obama's Universal Health Insurance Program.

Or imagine that your elderly father desperately needs an operation and one day, he calls you in distress. The treatment his doctor recommended was denied him. Why? Obama's Universal Health Insurance bureaucrats determined that his condition was not serious enough to justify the expense of the operation.

Appearing at hundreds of campaign events, Barack Obama often stands in front of banners that espouse "Change We Can Believe In." And his speeches usually include declarations like, "We want *change* in this country!" and, "The

American people are rising up and we're going to bring about *change* in this country!"

But what does he really mean when he says he wants "change"? What changes does he have in mind? America has her problems (what nation doesn't?), but what things are so awful and wrong that require the sort of radical "changes" Obama says we need?

If his life, his associations, and his personal behavior are any indication, such "changes" will not represent many of the principles upon which our great nation was founded. In fact, if Obama has his way—and gets a sympathetic Congress to boot—what remains may not be much of an America, at least not the country our fathers, grandfathers, and great-grandfathers fought to preserve.

"CHANGING" HEALTHCARE

Obama's approach to healthcare echoes an experiment of the 1990s: "HillaryCare." Obama proposes an expensive, government-controlled universal health plan that will dramatically lower that quality of care while making it more expensive.

Obama outlined his plan during the primary campaign, in a healthcare speech in Iowa:

> We now face an opportunity—and an obligation—to turn the page on the failed politics of yesterday's healthcare debates....
> My plan begins by covering every American. If you already have health insurance, the only thing that will change for you under this plan is the amount of money you will spend on premiums. That will be less. If you are one of the 45 million Americans who don't have health insurance, you will have it after this plan becomes law. No one will be turned away because of a preexisting condition or illness.[2]

Sounds good. His plan will provide coverage to Americans without health insurance and lower premiums for those who already have coverage. No rational American would oppose such a plan. But, as usual, the devil is in the details. For instance, as author, pundit, and political strategist Dick Morris notes:

> [Obama] wants to cover 12 million illegal immigrants with federally subsidized health insurance, dramatically driving up the costs and forcing federal rationing of healthcare. As in the U.K. and Canada, you will not be permitted certain medical procedures if the bureaucrats decide you are not worth it.[3]

And to help illegal aliens get access to taxpayer-funded healthcare, Obama wants to create new generations of Spanish-speaking Americans. Specifically, he wants all American children to be fluent in Spanish. As Obama said at a campaign stop in July 2008:

> I don't understand when people are going around worrying about, we need to have English only. They want to pass a law, we just, we want English only....

> But understand this, instead of worrying about whether immigrants can learn English, they'll learn English, you need to make sure your child can speak Spanish.

> You should be thinking about how can your child become bilingual. We should have every child speaking more than one language. It's embarrassing when Europeans come over here, they all speak English, they speak French, they speak German. And then we go over to Europe and all we can say is *merci beacoup*, right?[4]

On his campaign Web site, Obama makes some fairly accurate claims about the healthcare system in America today. Not enough of us are covered. In many respects the system is too expensive. Premiums are rising faster than wages. And so on.

To fix these problems, he says he will:

> [M]ake available a new national health plan to all Americans, including the self-employed and small businesses, to buy affordable health coverage that is similar to the plan available to members of Congress."[5]

According to Obama's Web site, the Congressional healthcare plan provides:[6]

"Guaranteed eligibility. No American will be turned away from any insurance plan because of illness or pre-existing conditions."

"Comprehensive benefits. The benefit package will be similar to that offered through Federal Employees Health Benefits Program (FEHBP), the plan members of Congress have. The plan will cover all essential medical services, including preventive, maternity and mental healthcare."

"Affordable premiums, co-pays and deductibles."

"Subsidies. Individuals and families who do not qualify for Medicaid or SCHIP but still need financial assistance will receive an income-related federal subsidy to buy into the new public plan or purchase a private healthcare plan."

"Simplified paperwork and reined in health costs."

Obama makes other claims, too. He says his plan will also offer "portability and choice," and for those wishing to purchase a private health insurance plan, Obama offers another government solution: the National Health Insurance Exchange, which "will act as a watchdog group and help reform the private insurance market by creating rules and standards for participating insurance plans to ensure fairness and to make individual coverage more affordable and accessible," according to a description of the plan on his Web site.[7] In other words, Obama would have Washington bureaucrats decide who is permitted to get certain medical treatments and operations.

Insurers would be forced to issue a policy to every applicant "and charge fair and stable premiums that will not depend upon health status," says Obama's Web site. "The Exchange will require that all the plans offered are at least as generous as the new public plan and have the same standards for quality and efficiency. The Exchange would evaluate plans and make the differences among the plans, including cost of services, public."

Meanwhile, employers who did not offer "meaningful" contributions to the cost of "quality health coverage" for their employees will be taxed "a percentage of payroll toward the costs of the national plan," says the description.

As Dr. John Goodman, founder and president of the National Center for Policy Analysis, explains:

> The Obama plan would subject all employers to a "pay-or-play" mandate—imposing a tax on those who do not provide health insurance for their employees. Following Commonwealth, we assume this would be a payroll tax of 7 percent of earnings up to $1.25 per hour on employers who fail to pay at least 75 percent of the premium for a minimum package of benefits...
>
> As the economics literature affirms, a payroll tax is almost completely born by workers themselves. During the Democratic party primary, Senator Obama criticized Senator Clinton's proposal to mandate coverage by asserting she would try to force people to buy something they cannot afford and then tax them when they don't buy it—leaving them worse off than they were. Exactly the same criticism applies to Obama's pay-or-play mandate.[8]

Goodman notes that the real beneficiaries of Obama's health care plan are likely to be the myriad special interest groups that feast on government mandated benefits:

> [S]tate regulations require insurers to cover all manner of procedures, ranging from acupuncture to *in vitro* fertilization, and providers, ranging from natureopaths to marriage counselors. These mandates reflect the lobbying power of special interests, and the resulting higher price of insurance causes as many as one-in-every-four uninsured people to be priced out of the market. By having the federal government impose a mandated benefit package, Obama would elevate this special interest feeding frenzy to the national level.[9]

To somehow streamline the healthcare system and lower costs, his plan also requires:

- More reporting from hospitals, clinics and medical facilities;

- More mandatory collection of data;

- Electronic medical records;

- Forced levels of coverage. Increased government oversight. A huge new government medical bureaucracy.

And who pays for all of this? Answer: *you.*

There is little debate that America's healthcare system is ill. It costs $2 trillion a year—the most of any industrialized nation. One-in-six dollars is spent on healthcare, and when the country's 65 million-plus baby boomers begin to retire, that amount is likely to increase to one-in-five.[10]

"Our healthcare system is in transition. It is unstable. It is unstable economically, and it is unstable politically. Economically, it is unstable because it is based on a system of insurance which is grounded in employment, and employment-based insurance in the United States is eroding," says Robert E. Moffit, PhD, in a 2006 analysis for the Heritage Foundation. "It is unstable politically because survey after survey shows that the American people are profoundly dissatisfied with the healthcare system, and majorities...will say that they are in favor of a massive overhaul in the system or major change in the system. Usually, the implicit suggestion is that they would like a system that looks like Great Britain or Canada or some other European country."[11]

According to Moffit, roughly fifty cents of every dollar we spend on healthcare "is now spent by the government," but, when the baby boomers retire, "the Medicare expansion will go into high gear."[12]

Rather than embracing our capitalistic system to repair the healthcare industry's most fundamental problems, Americans are moving in the opposite direction—led in part by healthcare hucksters such as Barack Obama.

REFUSING TO LEARN FROM OTHERS' MISTAKES

Obama and others like him, who support some kind of universal healthcare, often make their case by pointing to "success stories" in Canada and Europe, where such systems have been in place for some time now. But these government-run systems are a far cry from successful; in fact, learned observers and even medical practitioners within those systems have begun to speak out against them, because they are fatally flawed.

"Canadians are beginning to rethink their system. You find the same thing across Europe," says David Gratzer, M.D., a U.S.- and Canadian-based physician, senior fellow at the Manhattan Institute, and author of *Code Blue: Reviving Canada's Health Care System*.[13] As a physician in Canada, he says he began to rethink the country's healthcare system when he began noticing patients having to wait months and even years for otherwise routine medical tests, procedures, and surgeries. Oddly enough, however, he says he sees America heading down that same destructive path.

"[H]ere's the irony: If Canadians are willing to rethink things and embrace, at least to some extent, some capitalism when it comes to healthcare, I find increasingly that Americans are not," Gratzer says. "If Canadians are willing to rethink these issues, Americans are also rethinking and heading down the same lines that Canada once did. That's a terrible mistake."[14]

Unlike Obama and Co., Gratzer says the main reason why healthcare in the U.S. is so expensive is because Americans are *over*-insured, not under-insured. "As a result of this," he says,

"American healthcare is so terribly expensive because it's so terribly cheap.

The British are no better off, as Emmett Tyrrell, founder and editor of the *American Spectator*, a forty-year-old political and cultural magazine, points out:

> Health care officials in Britain discovered that patients were lingering in emergency rooms for days before being treated. Incensed by this, the bureaucrats magisterially ordered that emergency room patients be treated within four hours. The consequences were reported in the *Daily Mail*. Hundreds of "seriously ill patients" simply were kept longer in ambulances before being admitted to the emergency rooms. Hence, there were fewer ambulances available for subsequent emergencies. As Herzlinger notes, the consequence of socialized medicine is "rationing."[15]

According to Gratzer, employer coverage is one of the main influences in the rising cost of health insurance. On October 23, 1943, the IRS ruled for the first time that employers could provide their employees health insurance and pay the premiums in pre-tax dollars. The ruling came at a time of unprecedented price and wage controls during World War II; employers couldn't attract workers with better wages, so they opted to provide benefits (such as paid health insurance) instead. Over the years, Gratzer says, the benefit of employer-provided health insurance grew from basic coverage to covering "health" problems like sunglasses, marital counseling, and hair transplants, to name a few. As benefits grew, so did costs.

The implementation of government-paid insurance programs was another contributing factor. Medicare and Medicaid programs continue to grow at astronomical rates, and, when baby boomers begin to retire, Medicare will explode.

"The end result," Gratzer says, "is that Americans are just hopelessly over-insured when it comes to health insurance. For every dollar spent on healthcare in the United States, only fourteen cents comes out of pocket. That applies for people on Medicaid, Medicare, privately insured, and that's why we have such an upside-down universe when it comes to healthcare."[16]

And the worst is yet to come. According to Gratzer and other analysts, at some point between 2013 and 2017, depending on which analysis you believe, Medicare will begin spending more than it brings in. By about 2041—at the current and anticipated rates of expenditure—the program is expected to go broke.

"When today's college students reach retirement age in 2050, their children and grandchildren will face a payroll tax rate of about 16.8 percent to pay their Social Security benefits—a 37 percent increase over today's rate," says Matt Moore, a senior analyst at the National Center for Policy Analysis. "When Medicare Part A is included, the payroll tax burden will rise to 24.5 percent—almost one of every four dollars workers will earn that year."[17]

Obama's "prescription" for this problem is to add another huge government-run healthcare boondoggle financed by employers and the taxpayer. This program, too, will wind up going broke, after delivering sub-standard care to those whom it was ostensibly designed to help the most.

In a *Washington Post* article, Gratzer offered five solutions:[18]

- Make health insurance like other types of insurance by restructuring current health savings accounts (part of the 2003 Medicare reforms) and leveling the tax field for people not covered by an employer plan;

- Foster more competition through deregulation (healthcare is the most regulated sector in the American economy), in part by allowing consumers to shop around—even from state to state—for coverage;

- Reform Medicaid using the welfare reform template of allowing states to experiment and innovate with block grants provided by the federal government;

- Revisit Medicare reform, in part by scrapping price controls and using the Federal Employees Health Benefits Plan as a model—which would give elderly Americans a choice among competitive private sector plans;

- Address prescription drug prices by scaling back the scope of the Food and Drug Administration; it costs nearly a billion dollars for a new prescription drug to reach the market, and nearly 40 percent of that is safety regulations—essentially a massive tax on all pharmaceuticals.

Barack Obama rejected all of these suggestions. As part of his grand healthcare plan, he has said that doctors, hospitals, clinics, and medical laboratories will all have to provide more documentation (i.e., become more regulated) to "ensure quality care." The truth, however, is that *more* regulation won't guarantee quality of care. In fact, more regulation has led to less efficient, more expensive healthcare.

In their 2007 book, *Healthy Competition: What's Holding Back Health Care and How to Free It*, two experts from the libertarian Cato Institute argue that entitlements, tax laws, and costly regulations are hampering the U.S. healthcare system. According to a summary of the book, authors Michael F. Cannon, Cato's director of health policy studies, and Michael Tanner, director of health and welfare studies and the Project On on Social Security Choice, contend that "Consumer consumer choice and competition deliver higher quality and lower prices in other areas of the economy. The authors conclude that removing restrictions can do the same for healthcare."[19] Cannon and

Tanner argue that any reform method should expand patient choices and decision-making while dramatically *decreasing* choices and decisions made about patient healthcare by a bloated, faceless government bureaucracy.

"The answer then to America's healthcare problems lies not in heading down the road to national healthcare but in learning from the experiences of other countries, which demonstrate the failure of centralized command and control and the benefits of increasing consumer incentives and choice," writes Tanner, in a March 2008 Policy Analysis paper for Cato.[20] He says a closer examination of those systems shows that, to a program, all are "wrestling with problems of rising costs and lack of access to care," and that "the broad and growing trend" among nations with universal healthcare "is to move away from centralized government control and to introduce more market-oriented features."[21]

In other words, the global trend among nations with national healthcare programs is *just the opposite* of what Barack Obama is advocating—*less* centralized government control, not *more*. Why? Because these countries are learning that government produces the least efficient, least cost-effective product, and that free-market forces are much more suited to producing products that work at a reduced cost. "Countries with more effective national healthcare systems are successful to the degree that they incorporate market mechanisms such as competition, cost sharing, market prices, and consumer choice, and eschew centralized government control," says Tanner.[22]

Obama nonetheless has eschewed the free-market approach. He is convinced that the prescription to heal the ailing American healthcare system is more government, not less; more regulations, not fewer; more red tape, not less; more bureaucracy, not less. Meanwhile, experts agree that the free market—not Obama's big government solution—is the only thing that will save the U.S. healthcare system.

Less individual control and less personal freedom. Despite his rhetoric, that is Obama's vision of healthcare reform.

As a state senator in Illinois, Obama voted to require that dental anesthesia be covered by every health plan for difficult cases; today, that requirement is "one of forty-three mandates imposed by Illinois on health insurance, according to the Illinois Division of Insurance," writes Scott Gotlieb, a resident fellow at the American Enterprise Institute, in a May 2008 article for the *Wall Street Journal.*

"Other mandates require coverage of infertility treatments, drug rehab, 'personal injuries' incurred while intoxicated, and other forms of care." He continues:

> By my count, during Mr. Obama's tenure in the state senate, eighteen different laws came up for a vote and passed that imposed new mandates on private health insurance. Mr. Obama voted for all of them. As a presidential candidate, Mr. Obama says people lack health insurance because "they can't afford it." He's right. But he is also partly responsible for why health insurance is too expensive. A long list of studies show that mandates like the ones Mr. Obama has championed drive up the cost of insurance for the very people priced out of coverage.[23]

According to a 2008 study by the health insurance-supported industry, the Council for Affordable Health Insurance, mandates and government regulations are increasing the cost of insurance by 20 to -50 percent, depending on the state.[24]

"It doesn't have to be that way," writes Gottlieb. "If insurers were allowed to offer 'bare-bones' plans—which would be cheaper because they would cover just essential care—many consumers who are priced out of health insurance now would likely buy these plans instead of living without insurance." Again, the free market at work—but not in Obama's America.

"Socialism always means overriding the free decisions of individuals and replacing that capacity for decision making with an overarching plan by the state," writes Llewellyn Rockwell, president of the free-market Ludwig von Mises

Institute in Auburn, Alabama. "If you are serious about ending private ownership of the means of production, you have to be serious about ending freedom and creativity too."[25]

Welcome to Obama's America, where the answer to the nation's healthcare problems is more bloated, government bureaucracy.

For new, breaking information on Barack Obama since this book was published, please go to www.audacityofdeceit.com. If you have friends who would like to receive this chapter, or any of the chapters in this book, please refer them to the same Web site where they can download the chapter of their choice for free.

CHAPTER TEN

CHANGING AMERICAN DEFENSE

"Some seem to believe that we should negotiate with the terrorists and radicals, as if some ingenious argument will persuade them that they have been wrong all along. We have heard this foolish delusion before. As Nazi tanks crossed into Poland in 1939, an American senator declared: 'Lord, if I could only have talked to Hitler, all this might have been avoided.' We have an obligation to call this what it is: the false comfort of appeasement."[1]

—President George W. Bush, in a speech to the Israeli Knesset

W*HILE SERVICE* in the U.S. military has never been a requirement to hold the nation's highest elected office, it could be a critical factor in the current election cycle.

Our country remains fully engaged in a battle for a safe and secure future against what has accurately been described as a long-running war against an enemy practicing radical religious extremism. The September 11, 2001, attacks brought the brutality of our enemies to the forefront of our national psyche, but these Islamofascist enemies demonstrated their resolve years in advance, serving notice that they had declared war on our way of life with the first World Trade Center attack in 1993, the bombing of U.S. servicemen and women at Khobar Towers in Saudi Arabia in 1996, the twin attacks on U.S. embassies in Kenya and Tanzania in 1998, and the attack on the U.S.S. *Cole* in 2000.

But the assaults on American interests abroad and American citizens at home did not diminish until after 9/11, when the Bush administration finally took the fight to radical

Islamists such as Osama bin Laden. As of this writing, there has not been a single successful attack on American soil since 9/11, though terrorist attacks have succeeded around the world—in Spain, Germany, India, Israel, ColumbiaColombia, Russia, Thailand, the Philippines, Sri Lanka, Pakistan, Afghanistan, the United Kingdom, and Iraq. That doesn't mean there haven't been attempts, and it doesn't mean there won't be more in the future—some of which could very well be successful. But the point is, now is not the time to relax. Now is not the time to let down our guard. Now is *not* the time to appease our enemies.

Unfortunately, in Barack Obama, we have a 2008 presidential candidate whose national defense strategy apparently will do these very things. For Obama, "change" means handing the initiative in the Global War On on Terror (GWOT) *back* to our enemies.

How does Barack Obama propose dealing with the threat of more terrorism on our soil? His primary strategy, besides blaming the current administration for "not doing enough," is to support more gun control while opposing sensible national security measures.

NATIONAL SECURITY POLICY

Since 9/11, the Bush administration and Republicans in Congress have led the charge against our terrorist enemies by implementing a number of national security policies and passing new laws designed both to enhance our defenses against physical attack and to help intelligence agencies find the belligerents before they strike.

On the campaign trail, however, Obama has used a number of opportunities to bash the Bush administration for its alleged "abuse" of the Constitution, in pursuit of protecting the American homeland.

Specifically, Obama and his left-wing allies say they are "concerned" about changes in U.S. law enacted shortly after the 9/11 attacks that, in reality, took away a great deal of bureaucracy and red tape, making it *easier* for federal law enforcement and intelligence officials to monitor the actions of suspected *terrorists*. Imbodied in the "Uniting and Strengthening America by Providing Appropriate Tools Required to Intercept and Obstruct Terrorism Act of 2001" (the USA PATRIOT Act), the Bush administration—with the conscious consent of the majority of House and Senate members—proposed and passed the sweeping legislation designed to ensure America was never again caught unprepared by terrorists. Indeed, a summary of the Act reads: *"To deter and punish terrorist acts in the United States and around the world, to enhance law enforcement investigatory tools...."*[2]

An assessment of the Patriot Act by Kim R. Holmes, Ph.D., vice president of Foreign and Defense Policy Studies and director of the Kathryn and Shelby Cullom Davis Institute for International Studies at the Heritage Foundation, and Edwin Meese, III, President Ronald Reagan's closest advisor and a former U.S. attorney general in Reagan's administration, found that the legislation's impact on protecting the nation from future terrorist attacks was *invaluable* and *incalculable*:

> The changes in law contained in the administration's anti-terrorist proposal would be a small price to pay to enhance the nation's capabilities to apprehend terrorists. Whatever limited sacrifice in privacy and privileges there may be in these proposed measures is small in comparison to the long-term risks posed to civil liberties by terrorism. John Adams said in 1765 that "Liberty must at all hazards be supported. We have a right to it, derived from our Maker. But if we had not, our fathers have earned and bought it for us, at the expense of their ease, their estates, their pleasure, and their blood."... Americans will never be free so long as terrorists are threatening their homeland. It would be ironic indeed if an inordinate fear of losing some rights were sufficient to deny the nation the tools it needs to stop the very thing that would doom the Constitution

—the scourge of terrorism. Americans cannot be free unless they are secure any more than they, in the long run, can be secure unless they are free. The United States must stop terrorism in America if it is to preserve freedom.[3]

Holmes and Meese both agreed that, in order to best protect the nation, the debate could *not* be polarized into two camps, "one favoring security and the other favoring civil liberties":"[4]

> This can be accomplished in two ways. First, policymakers must distinguish between constitutional liberties on the one hand, and mere privileges and conveniences on the other. Second, they must understand that liberty depends on security and that freedom in the long run depends on eliminating the threat of terrorism as soon as possible.[5]

The scholars were also keenly aware that, in order to best preserve our constitutional republic, *all* lawmakers— regardless of party or political affiliation:

> Must do everything in their power to preserve the basic liberties protected by the U.S. Constitution, such as the due process of law (including the need to show probable cause and judicial review for issuing warrants and the right to a hearing); the right to be free of unreasonable search and seizures; the right of free speech and religion; and the right to assembly…
>
> However committed Americans must be to civil liberties, they do *not* have a constitutional right to complete privacy if it endangers the lives of others. Investigators should not be denied access to potentially critical information gained overseas by foreign intelligence sources that could save lives, merely because the methods by which it was obtained do not conform to the U.S. Constitution. Nor should sensitive intelligence information on terrorists be compromised by disclosure in open court proceedings. There must be a reasonable balance between privacy and security.[6]

In other words, the entire act was designed to thwart *terrorism*—it was never intended to be used against ordinary

American citizens and, as of this writing, has not been used for those purposes, regardless of what some Obama supporters charge. As President Bush stated in a speech before Ohio State Highway Patriot Academy graduates in June 2005:

> The Patriot Act closed dangerous gaps in America's law enforcement and intelligence capabilities—gaps the terrorists exploited when they attacked us on September the 11th.
>
> Since September the 11th, federal terrorism investigations have resulted in charges against more than 400 suspects, and more than half of those charged have been convicted. Federal, state, and local law enforcement have used the Patriot Act to break up terror cells in New York and Oregon and Virginia and in Florida. We've prosecuted terrorist operatives and supporters in California, in Texas, in New Jersey, in Illinois, and North Carolina and Ohio. These efforts have not always made the headlines, but they've made communities safer. The Patriot Act has accomplished exactly what it was designed to do—it has protected American liberty, and saved American lives."[7]

But how does Obama view the Act? In short, unfavorably. In his first bid for the U.S. Senate, Obama said on a 2003 Illinois National Organization for Women questionnaire that he would vote to "repeal the Patriot Act" or replace it with a "new, carefully crafted proposal." After he was elected to the Senate, he voted for a 2005 bill reauthorizing the Patriot Act— but it very easily could be considered a politically pragmatic vote for his future. That's because in December 2005, when the reauthorization bill first came up, he voted against ending debate—a position equivalent to declaring a lack of support for the measure.[8]

Obama's campaign Web site attempts to clear the record— as Obama sees it—by insinuating that he has always favored the Act. But a close examination of what he says versus what he actually believes demonstrates where his real sympathies lie. By his own admission, Obama's main focus on "improving" the act centers around "civil liberties protections." But neither he nor other Patriot Act critics ever produced any specific allegations of abuses under the law. In contrast, however, plenty of evidence indicates the Act is doing exactly what it was designed to do: protect Americans.

THE TRUTH ABOUT IRAQ

Before his election to the Senate and since, Obama has repeatedly assailed the Bush administration's wartime policies. Most of this criticism centered on the Iraq front in the Global War On on Terror (GWOT).

As he was gearing up for a U.S. Senate bid and *little more than a year* after Islamofascist zealots killed nearly three 3,000 Americans in New York City, Pennsylvania, and Virginia, Obama called the battle to secure America "a dumb war." On October 26, 2002, Barack Obama said:

> I don't oppose all wars. What I am opposed to is a dumb war. What I am opposed to is a rash war. What I am opposed to is the cynical attempt by Richard Perle and Paul Wolfowitz and other armchair, weekend warriors in this administration to shove their own ideological agendas down our throats, irrespective of the costs in lives lost and in hardships borne.[9]

Continuing this verbal assault during a Democratic presidential debate in Las Vegas in November 2007, Obama said:

> [T]he overall strategy is failed, because we have not seen any change in behavior among Iraq's political leaders.... That's why I'm going to bring this war to a close. That's why we can get our combat troops out within sixteen months and have to initiate the kind of regional diplomacy, not just talking to our friends, but talking to our enemies, like Iran and Syria, to try to stabilize the situation there."[10]

Obama's solution is to cut and run, to snatch defeat from the jaws of victory, and to abandon not just the Iraqi people but a crucial front in the GWOT.

Obama has said that, as president, he would disregard the advice of his generals—professional men and women who have spent all their adult lives studying, honing, and conducting combat operations under all sorts of battle conditions—and withdraw U.S. troops. If he wins the White House and keeps his promise, he will remove U.S. troops just as stability is beginning to take hold in Iraq.

But his cut-and-run strategy is no secret. Despite weak—if not pragmatic—efforts to hide it, Obama has maintained this "war strategy" since taking office. "Obama introduced a bill to begin troop redeployment in May of 2007 (it failed, as he must have known it would), but he has been critical of Rep. John Murtha's calls for a quick withdrawal," wrote Laura Flanders in *The Contenders*. "Again, that strategy: tacking slightly to the left while attacking the Left to make his position seem centrist. He was an early critic of the Iraq invasion, and in the most recent vote to cut off funding for the war he voted yes."[11]

In the meantime, Obama seemingly refuses to be honest with the American people, refuses to admit the truth about progress in Iraq—progress that was initiated by the U.S. invasion but that is now being accomplished, bit by bit, by the Iraqis themselves. Obama and his fellow Democrats are depending on failure in Iraq in advance of the 2008 general election, because they believe that failure will strengthen their position with the American people, that the invasion was ill-conceived, and that we need to change direction. Even if his assertions are wholly false, Obama focuses on failure, and nothing else.

"Both the *New York Times* and the *Washington Post* this week had front-page stories about successful operations by Iraqi forces to root out Shiite militias in Baghdad's Sadr City—a significant turning point in the war and a huge accomplishment for Iraqi Prime Minister Nouri al-Maliki," wrote columnist Linda Chavez in March 2008. "But there Obama was Tuesday evening…once again repeating the same old tired formulation about the 'failed'

Bush policy in Iraq, 'that asks everything of our troops and nothing of Iraqi politicians.'"[12]

Continuing her assessment, Chavez said Obama "certainly hasn't let the facts change his opinion about what is going on in Iraq or what the United States should do in response. Like a broken record, he just keeps repeating the same old tune. If he really were a new kind of politician, he'd cheer what's happening in Iraq, compliment Prime Minister Maliki for his strides, and rethink his promise to undercut the progress by a precipitous withdrawal of all American troops."[13]

Obama, with his broken-record rhetoric, reincarnates Vietnam War protestors who did everything they could to undercut U.S. success in that war; their prophecy became self-fulfilling when America finally abandoned its South Vietnamese allies and the regime fell to invading Communist forces from North Vietnam. Obama and the Democrats are doing much the same thing today, undercutting the U.S. effort in Iraq—pushing dates to withdraw troops, voting to cut military funding for Iraq, and more—because they hate George W. Bush, and because his failure is their victory.

Obama has disregarded other assessments of progress in Iraq. In March 2007—just a few months after the Pentagon ordered a "surge" of 30,000 troops to Iraq to quell mounting violence—retired U.S. Army officer Gordon Cucullu wrote, "'I walked down the streets of Ramadi a few days ago, in a soft cap eating an ice cream with the mayor on one side of me and the police chief on the other, having a conversation.' This simple act, Gen. David Petraeus told me, would have been 'unthinkable' just a few months ago. 'And nobody shot at us,' he added."[14]

Petraeus, the U.S. Army officer in charge of implementing the surge strategy, expounded on its success. Cucullu, writing in the *New York Post*, reported that although Petraeus was cautious and said, "We still have a long way to go," the top Iraq commander explained, "We got down at the people level and are staying…. Once the people know we are going to be around, then all kinds of things start to happen."[15] For example, more intelligence, was forthcoming—intelligence that U.S. forces used to find extremist hideouts, locate weapons caches, and learn about future plans to attack American forces.

Once, Petraeus said, U.S. forces were "scraping" for intelligence information. But after changing tactics and assuring the Iraquis of our continued presence, our troops began to get "information overload," a phenomenon of excess intelligence that commanders love. "After our guys are in the neighborhood for four or five days, the people realize they're not going to just leave them like we did in the past. Then they begin to come in with so much information on the enemy that we can't process it fast enough," said Petraeus.[16]

Concludes Cucullu: "Early signs are positive; early indicators say that we're winning. As Petraeus cautiously concluded, 'We'll be able to evaluate the situation for sure by late summer.' That's his job. Our job? *We need to give him the time and space needed to win this war* [emphasis added]."[17]

Several months later, in September, Petraeus—along with the U.S. ambassador to Iraq, Ryan Crocker—gave a similar assessment to members of Congress. For his part, Crocker reiterated Petraeus's assessment about needing time to complete the mission, with an important caveat: "Iran plays a harmful role in Iraq. Our current course is hard. The alternatives are far worse."[18] In other words, if the U.S. leaves too soon, before Iraq is stable—as Obama is advocating—all will have been for naught. Iran will step into the vacuum we leave behind and a fledgling democracy that would have been a huge U.S. ally in the region will have failed to take root.

PRE-WAR INTELLIGENCE

In fact, Obama has been wrong about Iraq from the beginning— the beginning of the war and even since the beginning of his U.S. Senate campaign.

Prior to the U.S. invasion in March 2003, American and Western intelligence agencies shared a widely held belief that Saddam Hussein was a grave threat to the United States and the surrounding region. With 9/11 still fresh in Americans' minds, the White House responsibly concluded it could not ignore this threat. That wasn't just George W. Bush's belief, nor just the belief of U.S. intelligence agencies. Almost everyone in the international intelligence community also believed that Saddam Hussein's Iraq posed a grave danger to the United States.

The Bush administration's "perception of Saddam's weapons capacities was shared by the Clinton administration, congressional Democrats, and most other Western governments and intelligence services," writes Paul R. Pillar, a career CIA officer who served as the National Intelligence Officer for the Near East and South Asia from 2000 to 2005.[19] While acknowledging that the administration's decision to invade Iraq was based on flawed evidence, that was the information that was available at the time the Bush administration made the decision.

Michael Barone, a resident fellow at the American Enterprise Institute, made the same case, adding that critics of the administration's decision—including Obama—charge the White House "politicized" the Iraq pre-war intelligence to justify the war. Further, he said, intelligence and data discovered and released a few years after the invasion was "a step forward" in discovering what factors led to it. In detailing information in the book, *War and Decision*, by Douglas Feith—the number-three civilian at the Pentagon from 2001 to 2005—Barone wrote in a May 2008 column, "The picture Feith paints is at considerable variance from the narratives with which we've become familiar."[20]

Feith, Barone said, laid waste to a number of misconceptions and outright fabrications that critics such as Obama have associated with the Iraq front in the GWOT:

One such narrative is, "Bush lied; people died." The claim is that "neocons," including Feith, politicized intelligence to show that Saddam Hussein's regime had weapons of mass destruction. Not so, as the Senate Intelligence Committee and the Silberman-Robb Commission have concluded already. Every intelligence agency believed Saddam had weapons of mass destruction, and the post-invasion Duelfer report concluded that he maintained the capability to produce them on short notice. There was abundant evidence of contacts between Saddam's regime and al-Qaeda and other terrorist groups. Given Saddam's hostility to the United States and his stonewalling of the United Nations, American leaders had every reason to believe he posed a grave threat. Removing him removed that threat.[21]

The biggest error committed by the administration, however, was letting opponents like Obama frame the debate once it became known that stockpiles of weapons of mass destruction did not exist. Barone continues:

Unfortunately—and here Feith is critical of his ultimate boss, George W. Bush—the administration allowed its critics to frame the issue around the fact that stockpiles of weapons weren't found. Here we see at work the liberal fallacy, apparent in debates on gun control, that weapons are the problem rather than the people with the capability and will to use them to kill others. The fact that millions of law-abiding Americans have guns is not a problem; the problem is that criminals can get them and have the will to kill others. Similarly, the fact that France has WMDs is not a problem; the fact that Saddam Hussein had the capability to produce WMDs and the will to use them against us was.[22]

Feith also hits Bush and his administration for not effectively defending the rationale for the invasion—which was to protect Americans from a genuine threat of state-sponsored terrorism—and focusing instead on the "iffy goal of establishing democracy."[23]

Finally, in a pathetic bid to justify his own views and pacify the constituency that supported him through the primary season, Obama mischaracterizes his opponent's views on the war, claiming that Senator John McCain wants to keep American troops fighting in Iraq for "a hundred years." This lie is based on a statement McCain made in response to a debate question in January 2008:

> **Questioner:** President Bush has talked about our staying in Iraq for fifty years...
>
> **McCain:** Maybe one hundred. Make it one hundred. We've been in South Korea, we've been in Japan for sixty years. We've been in South Korea for fifty years or so. That'd be fine with me as long as Americans are not being injured or harmed or wounded or killed. Then it's fine with me. I would hope it would be fine with you if we maintain a presence in a very volatile part of the world where Al Qaeda is training, recruiting, equipping and motivating people every single day.

"It's clear from this that McCain isn't saying he'd support continuing the war for one hundred years, only that it might be necessary to keep troops there that long. That's a very different thing," stated the *Columbia Journalism Review* in a spot-on analysis of McCain's statement. "As he says, we've had troops in South Korea for over fifty years, but few people think that means we're still fighting the Korean War."[24]

APPEASING TERRORISTS

Even when he's not ostensibly being dishonest about defending America, Obama signals the terms of his overall foreign policy, and all the signs indicate that he would set a dangerous precedent with a policy that amounts to nothing more than appeasing America's sworn enemies.

During a CNN/*YouTube.com* Democratic debate in July 2007, Obama and rival Senator Hillary Clinton—both of whom have heavily criticized the Bush administration's approach to foreign policy—were asked if they, as president, would be willing to meet with leaders of such rogue states as Iran, Venezuela, Cuba and North Korea. Obama readily said that not only would he do so, he would do so in his *first year* of office.

Claiming "it is a disgrace we have not spoken to them," Obama added, "The notion that somehow not talking to countries is punishment to them—which has been the guiding diplomatic principle of this administration—is ridiculous."[25]

Apparently unbeknownst to Obama, it is not "ridiculous" to deny our enemies the upper hand at all times, especially in negotiations. To do so is not a "punishment," and American diplomacy is not based on kindergarten rules. It would be a "disgrace," however, to allow a lesser power to dictate terms to the most powerful country on the planet.

In diplomatic speak, Obama's approach is called "appeasement." And as history has demonstrated, it doesn't work.

In fact, it has been U.S. policy for decades—through Republican *and* Democratic administrations—*not* to appease rogue nations—nations that (a) sponsor terrorism (think Venezuela and Iran); or (b) attempt to hold U.S. foreign policy and that of its allies hostage (think Iran and North Korea, via their nuclear weapons programs). Negotiations, when they have taken place, have usually been through third-party intermediaries or in conjunction with other nations, though in the case of Cuba (the Clinton administration) and North Korea (the Bush administration), the U.S. did occasionally hold certain high-level direct talks, depending on the importance of the issue. The reason is simple: as a superpower, the U.S. cannot afford to look weak before the world by appearing to kowtow to a lesser enemy or adversary. To do so would encourage smaller, less powerful nations to do the same and, worse, stronger enemies would feel empowered to take a more hostile approach to the U.S., thinking they can get away with such affronts. This isn't rocket science; it's Diplomacy 101.

A perfect example of why it is criminally naïve, as well as inherently dangerous to our national security, for Obama to make such outrageous comments about appeasing our enemies is evident in the 1994 Agreed Framework deal—the last great act of appeasement struck by the Clinton administration. This agreement—negotiated between North Korea, South Korea, Japan, and the U.S.—was aimed at rewarding Pyongyang for abandoning its atomic weapons production program. But under the Stalinist dictatorship of Kim Jong-il Il, North Korea continued to secretly develop its nuclear capability—a capability it finally admitted in 2002, after the Bush administration confronted Kim's government with irrefutable evidence.[26] "Talking" to North Korea hadn't accomplished a thing; in fact, all it did was buy time for the regime in Pyongyang to develop its program in secret. North Korea tested its first nuclear weapon in 2006, making it the latest member state to join the nuclear club.

Iran is now at a similar juncture. Assisted by Russia, the Islamic regime in Tehran is racing to develop its own nuclear weapons capability—one that its religious extremist government has threatened to use repeatedly against Israel (which reportedly has its own nuclear weapons capability). Elected as Iran's president in 2005, Mahmoud Ahmadinejad has denied the Holocaust and repeatedly called for Israel to be "wiped off the map," while his country moves ever closer to obtaining a functioning nuclear weapons capability.[27]

Furthermore, Iran, in supplying Iraq- and Afghanistan-based militants with weapons and training, is responsible for the deaths of U.S. soldiers. According to a *Washington Post* report in June 2007, "Iran has increased arms shipments to both Iraq's Shiite extremists and Afghanistan's Taliban in recent weeks in an apparent attempt to pressure American and other Western troops operating in its two strategic neighbors, according to senior U.S. and European officials."[28]

Such weapons include 240mm rockets, 107mm mortars, rocket-propelled grenades, C-4 explosives, and small arms.[29]

What is Obama's solution to this act of war? He wants to "talk"—to a rogue nation whose government has a hand in killing American soldiers, sailors, airmen, and Marines. Whether Obama thinks the Iraq front of the GWOT is necessary or not, what is *absolutely true* is that the U.S. has done *nothing* to Iran that would justify this Muslim extremist regime placing weapons into the hands of our enemies in Iraq.

Can America survive a president who is naïve? Can we survive a leader who is afraid to stand on *our* terms in the face of terrorists, tyrants, and dictators? While the job requires that the president defend our country and protect our fighting men and women, Obama says getting tough with terrorists is the more dangerous course. He says, "We live in a more dangerous world, partly as a consequence of Bush's actions, primarily because of this war in Iraq that should have never been authorized or waged."[30] But, by any measure, the Bush administration's brand of foreign policy—dealing swiftly and effectively with our enemies—is the much more successful approach.

As of this writing—seven years after 9/11—*no new terrorist attacks* have been carried out on U.S. soil since President Bush launched the GWOT. Yet, according to Obama, our most visible terrorist enemy—al Qaeda—is *more* powerful *now* than in the days when its extremist minions were hijacking U.S. airliners, attacking American warships, and detonating car bombs in the middle of New York City.

"We are seeing al-Qaeda stronger now than at any time since 2001. That is a significant threat that has to be dealt with. Because we have been distracted, we have ended up seeing a more dangerous situation," Obama said during a Democratic presidential debate hosted by the Congressional Black Caucus.[31]

He is virtually alone in that assessment. While it's true the extremist organization remains a threat, both in Iraq and abroad, al-Qaeda is a shell of what it once was, as evidenced by its inability to launch anything but the most primitive, roadside attacks in our current GWOT theaters of operation.

Still, despite this success—and in conjunction with his appeasement strategy—Obama's military policy is to cut and run, though, in doing so, even *he* admits it is a dicey approach that is sure to be used against us.

"What the militias are essentially doing is they've just pulled back. They've said as long as there's increased troop presence, we'll lie low, we'll wait it out. As soon as the Americans start leaving and redeploying into other areas, we will come back in," he said on CNN's *Larry King Live*.[32]

While he supports immediate withdrawal from Iraq, Obama simultaneously admits that our enemies would simply "lie low" until U.S. forces left. What does this say about our potential commander-in-chief, who knows his strategy is flawed before he implements it, but would embark on it anyway?

Further confusing his military strategy, Obama has also said the U.S. should avoid a "precipitous withdrawal" of American forces that is ultimately driven by "congressional edict."

"[H]aving visited Iraq, I'm also acutely aware that a precipitous withdrawal of our troops, driven by congressional edict rather than the realities on the ground, will not undo the mistakes.... It *could compound them* [emphasis added]. It could compound them by plunging Iraq into an even deeper and, perhaps, irreparable crisis," he said in 2006.[33]

Of course, that's true. So why has Obama consistently been calling for a "precipitous withdrawal" throughout his campaign?

Obama clearly does not have a clue about what it takes to keep a great nation like ours safe. Certainly, diplomacy has its place, but not when an enemy is actively engaged against us. We will have plenty of time to "talk" to the enemy—*after* we've subdued him, not before—otherwise we may find ourselves hostage to our enemy's terms. Appeasement, cutting and running from a fight, and leaving our enemies with the upper hand are recipes for failure in a war we cannot afford to lose.

"There is no safety for the weak and foolish," wrote former New York City mayor Ed Koch. "When you seek to end a war without substantially achieving your essential goals by simply ceasing to fight, it is often a form of surrender."[34]

Welcome to Obama's America, where victory in the Global War on Terror will slip away, lost to an ill-conceived strategy and a dedicated, extremist enemy to whom we will surrender first—and apologize later.

For new, breaking information on Barack Obama since this book was published, please go to www.audacityofdeceit.com. If you have friends who would like to receive this chapter, or any of the chapters in this book, please refer them to the same Web site where they can download the chapter of their choice for free.

CHAPTER ELEVEN

THE BARACK OBAMA TEST

"I'm asking you to believe. Not just in my ability to bring about real change in Washington... I'm asking you to believe in yours."

—Obama '08 Presidential Campaign Website

Y*EARS AGO*, a very good friend of mine, Victor Kamber, and I wrote two books: *Are You a Conservative or a Liberal*, and *"Are You a Republican or a Democrat."* Both were tremendously successful and popular, and serve as the inspiration for this chapter.

Americans rushed to tell us how wonderful these political ideology tests were for driving discussion and interest in politics with their students, children, and friends. Families took the test together, provoking lively debates at the dinner table. Husbands and wives took the tests and discovered things they didn't know about each other. Teachers who gave the tests to their students told me how amazed they were at not only the results, but also how the tests provoked interesting and thoughtful classroom discussions and debates among otherwise disinterested students.

Even Rush Limbaugh took the tests, as did many prominent Liberals. Rush also read the tests over the air to his 20 million listeners so they, too, could take them.

The tests were so popular that *USA Weekend* magazine invited Vic Kamber and I to put them on the magazine's cover before two elections in the '90s.

Now, the reason I wrote this book is because I have six children and five voting-age grandchildren—and some of them have told me that Obama's philosophy appeals to them, but they don't really know what he stands for.

So I created the following test for them to take, for you to take, and for any of your friends or family members, who might be considering voting for Barack Obama, to take.

Here is how it works.

Ask yourself each of the poll questions below. Each time you side with the Obama position, give yourself one point. Each time you do not side with the Obama position, subtract one point.

Once you have completed all the questions, look at your score. If you score in the positive range, you should vote for Obama. However, if you score in the negative range, then you need to seriously consider if his positions are really what you want for America over the next four years.

The polling results we've gathered are from America's most reputable pollsters in the business, including Zogby International, Rasmussen, Gallup Organization, and Opinion Research. They suggest that Americans are simply not buying into Obama's program of change. Although Americans may like the message of "change," they clearly disagree with Obama's policies for "change."

Of course, Obama is in the midst of constantly changing his positions; however, the positions below are those that he has held most of his adult life.

Good luck!

SOCIAL VALUES

Should a doctor give medical care to a fetus that survives an abortion, or should medical care not be given?

		All Americans	Female
Obama Position ▶	Should Not	17.7%	18.6%
	Should	67.8%	68.1%
	Not Sure	14.5%	13.2%

(Source: Associated Television News/Zogby America Poll of 1,005 likely voters conducted 7/9/08 through 7/14/08. Margin of Error +/- 3.2 percentage points)

Do you favor or oppose a woman's right to an abortion based on the sex of the fetus?

		All Americans	Female
Obama Position ▶	Favor	12.3%	9.1%
	Oppose	82.2%	87.5%
	Not Sure	5.5%	3.4%

(Source: Associated Television News/Zogby America Poll of 1,005 likely voters conducted 7/9/08 through 7/14/08. Margin of Error +/- 3.2 percentage points

Do you agree or disagree that a physician should be legally required to notify the parents of an underage girl who requests an abortion?

		All Americans	Female
	Agree	77.0%	73.5%
Obama Position ▶	Disagree	17.0%	22.5%
	Not Sure	3.4%	3.9%

(Source: Associated Television News/Zogby America Poll of 1,005 likely voters conducted 7/9/08 through 7/14/08. Margin of Error +/- 3.2 percentage points)

Do you agree or disagree that abortion destroys a human life and is manslaughter?

		All Americans	Female
	Agree	51.5%	55.5%
Obama Position ▶	Disagree	39.8%	36.6%
	Not Sure	8.7%	7.9%

(Source: Associated Television News/Zogby America Poll of 1,005 likely voters conducted 7/9/08 through 7/14/08. Margin of Error +/- 3.2 percentage points)

Do you believe that human life begins at conception, or once the baby may be able to survive outside the mother's womb with medical assistance, or when the baby is actually born?

	All Americans
At conception	55.0%
Survive outside womb	23.0%
Obama Position ▶ Not Sure	9.0%

(Source: Associated Television News/Zogby America Poll of 1,005 likely voters conducted 7/9/08 through 7/14/08. Margin of Error +/- 3.2 percentage points)

In general, what should be more important to Americans in their daily life: Moral values or material concerns?

	All Americans
Moral Values	88.0%
Obama Position ▶ Material Concerns	6.1%
Not Sure	5.9%

(Source: Associated Television News/Zogby America Poll of 1,005 likely voters conducted 7/9/08 through 7/14/08. Margin of Error +/- 3.2 percentage points)

Should America's laws be written following Judeo-Christian values or should America be an entirely secular society, devoid of any decisions based upon Judeo-Christian moral values?

		All Americans
	Judeo-Christian values	44.4%
Obama Position ▶	Secular society	40.3%
	Not Sure	5.9%

(Source: Associated Television News/Zogby America Poll of 1,005 likely voters conducted 7/9/08 through 7/14/08. Margin of Error +/- 3.2 percentage points)

Which comes closest to your view on abortion: abortion should always be legal, or should be legal most of the time, or should be made illegal except in cases of rape, incest and to save the mother's life, or abortion should be made illegal without any exceptions?

		All Americans
Obama Position ▶	Always legal	31.0%
	Legal most of the time	13.0%
	Illegal with a few exceptions	40.0%
	Illegal without exceptions	10.0%
	Unsure	6.0%

(*Los Angeles Times*/Bloomberg Poll. Oct. 19-22, 2007. N=1039 registered voters nationwide. MoE ± 3. RV = registered voters)

Now I would like to ask your opinion about a specific abortion procedure known as late-term abortion or partial-birth abortion, which is sometimes performed on women during the last few months of pregnancy. Do you think that the government should make this procedure illegal, or do you think that the procedure should be legal?

		All Americans
	Illegal	66.0%
Obama Position ▶	Legal	28.0%
	Unsure	5.0%

(CNN/Opinion Research Corporation Poll. May 4-6, 2007. N=1,028 adults nationwide. MoE ± 3.)

SECOND AMENDMENT

Do you agree or disagree that American firearm manufacturers who sell a legal product that is not defective should be sued if a criminal uses their products in a crime?

		All Americans
Obama Position ▶	Agree	13.9%
	Disgree	76.2%

(Zogby Interactive Post Election Poll conducted 11/3-16/2004 of 36,581 voters. Margin of error + 0.5)

Currently, thirty-six states have laws that allow residents to qualify for a permit to carry a firearm if they pass a background check, if they take a firearms safety-training course, and if they pay a fee to cover administrative costs. Do you support or oppose such laws?

		All Americans
	Support	77.6%
Obama Position ▶	Oppose	14.8%

(Zogby Interactive Post Election Poll conducted 11/3-16/2004 of 36,581 voters. Margin of error + 0.5)

A. There needs to be new and tougher gun control laws to help in the fight against gun crime. B. There are enough laws on the books. What is needed is better enforcement of current gun control laws.

		All Americans
Obama Position ▶	Statement A	35.1%
	Statement B	60.0%
	Not Sure	4.9%

(Zogby Interactive Post Election Poll conducted 11/3-16/2004 of 36,581 voters. Margin of error + 0.5)

Would you favor or oppose a law that banned the sale of handguns?

		All Americans
Obama Position ▶	Favor	36.0%
	Oppose	59.0%
	Not Sure	5.0%

(Pew Research Center for the People & the Press survey conducted by Abt SRBI. April 23-27, 2008. N=1,502 adults nationwide. MoE ± 3.)

FELON VOTING

Do you agree or disagree that laws prohibiting convicted felons and non-US citizens from voting should be more vigorously enforced?

		All Americans
	Agree	70.1%
Obama Position ▶	Disagree	21.0%

(Zogby Interactive Post Election Poll conducted 11/3-16/2004 of 36,581 voters. Margin of error + 0.5)

TAXES

Do you favor or oppose an increase in the tax that stock holders pay on returns from 15 percent to nearly 40 percent?

		All Americans	70% who pay taxes	30% who don't pay taxes
Obama Position ▶	Favor	25.6%	22.6%	34.0%
	Oppose	65.9%	58.5%	68.6%

(Source: Associated Television News/Zogby America Poll of 1,005 likely voters conducted 7/9/08 through 7/14/08. Margin of Error +/- 3.2 percentage points)

Do you favor or oppose increasing the death tax rate to 55 percent for any income past the first $1 million?

		All Americans	70% who pay taxes	30% who don't pay taxes
Obama Position ▶	Favor	37.0%	36.0%	39.6%
	Oppose	52.6%	55.4%	46.0%

(Source: Associated Television News/Zogby America Poll of 1,005 likely voters conducted 7/9/08 through 7/14/08. Margin of Error +/- 3.2 percentage points)

Do you favor or oppose raising the top tax rate on the self-employed from 37.9 percent to 54.9 percent?

		All Americans	70% who pay taxes	30% who don't pay taxes
Obama Position ▶	Favor	10.5%	7.4%	18.6%
	Oppose	84.5%	88.6%	74.3%

(Source: Associated Television News/Zogby America Poll of 1,005 likely voters conducted 7/9/08 through 7/14/08. Margin of Error +/- 3.2 percentage points)

America's 3.7 million Sub Chapter S corporations, which are small companies with less than seventy-five stockholders, are currently taxed at a rate of 35 percent. Do you favor or oppose increasing the tax rate on these businesses to 50.3 percent?

		All Americans	70% who pay taxes	30% who don't pay taxes
Obama Position ▶	Favor	8.7%	7.9%	10.8%
	Oppose	85.4%	87.4%	80.8%

(Source: Associated Television News/Zogby America Poll of 1,005 likely voters conducted 7/9/08 through 7/14/08. Margin of Error +/- 3.2 percentage points)

How much should Americans who earn $1 million per year pay in federal income taxes?

		All Americans	70% who pay taxes	30% who don't pay taxes
	35% or less	57.7%	50.1%	52.3%
Obama Position ▶	35% or more	33.2%	33.1%	33.4%
	Not sure	15.1%	14.7%	16.3%

(Source: Associated Television News/Zogby America Poll of 1,005 likely voters conducted 7/9/08 through 7/14/08. Margin of Error +/- 3.2 percentage points)

How much should someone who wins $1 million in the lottery pay in federal income tax?

		All Americans	70% who pay taxes	30% who don't pay taxes
	35% or less	67.5%	66.3%	70.4%
Obama Position ▶	35% or more	22.0%	23.7%	16.9%
	Not sure	10.7%	10.0%	12.6%

(Source: Associated Television News/Zogby America Poll of 1,005 likely voters conducted 7/9/08 through 7/14/08. Margin of Error +/- 3.2 percentage points)

Tell me which of the following top individual tax rates, which combine income and social security, do you think is most fair?

	All Americans	70% who pay taxes	30% who don't pay taxes
28% (Under Reagan)	48.5%	51.2%	32.8%
38% (Under Clinton)	27.7%	24.4%	36.1%
Obama Position ▶ 55% (Obama)	12.1%	10.3%	16.5%
60% (Under Hoover)	.9%	1.0%	.7%
70% (Under Johnson, Carter)	2.6%	2.1%	4.1%
Not sure	10.9%	11.0%	9.9%

(Source: Associated Television News/Zogby America Poll of 1,005 likely voters conducted 7/9/08 through 7/14/08. Margin of Error +/- 3.2 percentage points)

According to the Tax Policy Center, Barack Obama's tax plans would cost the U.S federal government nearly $900 billion in his first term, and increase the national debt by $3.3 trillion over ten years. Do you believe the analysis that Obama's plans will be too costly for the U.S., or do you think the changes are needed?

	All Americans	70% who pay taxes	30% who don't pay taxes
Too costly	50.8%	54.3%	41.5%
Obama Position ▶ Needed	35.8%	33.1%	42.6%
Not sure	13.4%	12.5%	15.8%

(Source: Associated Television News/Zogby America Poll of 1,005 likely voters conducted 7/9/08 through 7/14/08. Margin of Error +/- 3.2 perc.entage points.)

Some say Obama's proposed increase in deductions for taxpayers would increase the number of those who don't pay taxes closer to 40 percent. Do you agree or disagree with Obama's proposed increase in deductions?

	All Americans	70% who pay taxes	30% who don't pay taxes
Obama Position ▶ Agree	7.5%	33.3%	48.5%
Disagree	47.3%	50.9%	37.9%
Not sure	15.2%	15.8%	13.6%

(Source: Associated Television News/Zogby America Poll of 1,005 likely voters conducted 7/9/08 through 7/14/08. Margin of Error +/- 3.2 percentage points)

Did you not have to pay any taxes last year because your income level was below the threshold to pay taxes or because your tax deductions left you with no liability?

	All Americans
I did not have to pay any taxes	29.0%
I had to pay taxes	69.3%

(Source: Associated Television News/Zogby America Poll of 1,005 likely voters conducted 6/27/08 through 6/30/08. Margin of Error +/- 3.2 percentage points)

ENERGY

Presently, 85 percent of American energy comes from fossil fuels while 7 percent comes from alternative energy sources. Do you support or oppose increasing taxes on fossil fuels in an effort to force our nation to increase its reliance on alternative or renewable energy sources and reducing environmental pollution—even if doing so would mean the taxes are eventually passed on to the consumer?

	<u>All Americans</u>
Obama Position ▶ Support tax increase on fossil fuels	35.5%
Oppose tax increase on fossil fuels	60.9%
Not sure	3.7%

(Source: Associated Television News/Zogby America Poll of 1,005 likely voters conducted 7/9/08 through 7/14/08. Margin of Error +/- 3.2 percentage points)

Proponents of drilling in the Arctic National Wildlife Refuge in Alaska point out that drilling could cover an area that covers 2,000 of the total 19 million acres that make up ANWR. Should the U.S. begin drilling in ANWR even if we won't realize the potential benefit for several more years?

	<u>All Americans</u>
Yes	54.1%
Obama Position ▶ No	36.3%
Not sure	9.6%

(Source: Associated Television News/Zogby America Poll of 1,005 likely voters conducted 7/9/08 through 7/14/08. Margin of Error +/- 3.2 percentage points)

Until recently, the U.S. has maintained a moratorium on oil drilling off our coasts. Should the U.S. begin drilling for oil fifty miles off our shores, as China is doing in cooperation with Cuba, even if the U.S. won't realize the potential benefits for another one to three years?

		All Americans
	Yes	68.1%
Obama Position ▶	No	23.4%
	Not sure	8.5%

(Source: Associated Television News/Zogby America Poll of 1,005 likely voters conducted 6/27/08 through 6/30/08. Margin of Error +/- 3.2 percentage points)

Some say Barack Obama's plans to implement sweeping environmental regulations will raise the cost of gas, groceries, heating, and air conditioning. Do you favor or oppose Obama's environmental plans?

		All Americans	70% who pay taxes	30% who don't pay taxes
Obama Position ▶	Favor	32.5%	31.3%	34.8%
	Oppose	49.1%	51.5%	43.4%
	Not sure	18.4%	17.2%	21.8%

(Source: Associated Television News/Zogby America Poll of 1,005 likely voters conducted 7/9/08 through 7/14/08. Margin of Error +/- 3.2 percentage points)

The U.S. currently adds a tariff of fifty-four cents on each gallon of imported ethanol from countries like Brazil in an effort to protect American companies producing ethanol from corn. The tariff is passed on to the consumer in the form of higher fuel prices. Should this tariff on imported ethanol...

		All Americans
Obama Position ▶	Continue	30.1%
	Be eliminated	61.9%
	Not sure	8.0%

(Source: Associated Television News/Zogby America Poll of 1,005 likely voters conducted 7/9/08 through 7/14/08. Margin of Error +/- 3.2 percentage points)

There are 104 nuclear reactors in the US today that produce 20 percent of America's energy needs and no accident has occurred at these reactors in thirty years. Other nations, such as France, are far more reliant on nuclear power, as 77 percent of that nation's electricity comes from nuclear sources. How much of America's energy needs would you like to see nuclear reactors meet?

		All Americans
	Generate 2%	5.2%
	Generate 10%	5.3%
	Generate 20%	12.0%
	Generate as much energy as possible from nuclear power	58.6%
Obama Position ▶	No power from nuclear reactors	12.8%
	Not sure	6.2%

(Source: Associated Television News/Zogby America Poll of 1,005 likely voters conducted 7/9/08 through 7/14/08. Margin of Error +/- 3.2 percentage points)

JUSTICE

In general, do you think the current Supreme Court is too liberal, too conservative, or just about right?

		All Americans
	Too Liberal	21.0%
Obama Position ▶	Too Conservative	32.0%
	About Right	43.0
	No Opinion	5.0%

(Gallup Poll conducted September 14-16, 2007)

HEALTHCARE

Do you agree or disagree with Barack Obama's $65 billion plan to institute taxpayer-funded universal health coverage, which would provide health insurance for those currently uninsured, including illegal immigrants?

		All Americans	70% who pay taxes	30% who don't pay taxes
Obama Position ▶	Agree	35.1%	31.0%	46.5%
	Disagree	59.9%	65.1%	45.5%
	Not sure	5.0%	3.9%	8.0%

(Source: Associated Television News/Zogby America Poll of 1,005 likely voters conducted 7/9/08 through 7/14/08. Margin of Error +/- 3.2 percentage points)

Should federally subsidized health insurance pay for healthcare for America's 12 million illegal immigrants?

		All Americans	70% who pay taxes	30% who don't pay taxes
Obama Position ▶	Yes	18.2%	15.0%	26.7%
	No	78.1%	81.3%	69.5%
	Not sure	3.7%	3.8%	3.8%

(Source: Associated Television News/Zogby America Poll of 1,005 likely voters conducted 7/9/08 through 7/14/08. Margin of Error +/- 3.2 percentage points)

TRADE

Some say Barack Obama's plan to raise taxes and increase trade barriers are similar to those created by President Herbert Hoover in the 1930s, which contributed to worsening America's economy. Do you think Obama's plans will worsen the economy as well, or do you think they will help the economy?

		All Americans	70% who pay taxes	30% who don't pay taxes
	Worsen	49.8%	52.9%	41.7%
Obama Position ▶	Help	34.1%	33.6%	36.0%
	Not sure	16.1%	13.5%	22.3%

(Source: Associated Television News/Zogby America Poll of 1,005 likely voters conducted 7/9/08 through 7/14/08. Margin of Error +/- 3.2 percentage points)

DEFENSE

Do you agree or disagree that Homeland Security should have to seek out a warrant in federal court in order to perform search and seizure on a non-citizen on American soil suspected of being involved in terrorism?

		All Americans
Obama Position ▶	Agree	41.9%
	Disagree	56.1%
	Not sure	2.0%

(Source: Associated Television News/Zogby America Poll of 1,005 likely voters conducted 7/9/08 through 7/14/08. Margin of Error +/- 3.2 percentage points)

Do you agree or disagree that Homeland Security should have to seek out a warrant in federal court in order to perform search and seizure on an American citizen suspected of being involved in terrorism?

		All Americans
Obama Position ▶ Agree		63.2%
Disagree		33.5%
Not sure		3.3%

(Source: Associated Television News/Zogby America Poll of 1,005 likely voters conducted 7/9/08 through 7/14/08. Margin of Error +/- 3.2 percentage points)

Should someone who is not a U.S. citizen, being held under suspicion of terrorism, be afforded Constitutional rights?

		All Americans
Obama Position ▶ Yes		30.1%
No		64.0%
Not sure		5.7%

(Source: Associated Television News/Zogby America Poll of 1,005 likely voters conducted 7/9/08 through 7/14/08. Margin of Error +/- 3.2 percentage points)

Should the U.S. negotiate with Iran without preconditions?

		All Americans
Obama Position ▶ Yes		21.0%
No		62.5%
Not sure		6.5%

(Source: Associated Television News/Zogby America Poll of 1,005 likely voters conducted 7/9/08 through 7/14/08. Margin of Error +/- 3.2 percentage points)

If American deaths in Iraq are greatly reduced and stability has returned to the Iraqi government, should American troops withdraw in eighteen months, or should they withdraw gradually over a longer timeframe?

	All Americans
Obama Position ▶ Withdraw in eighteen months	43.6%
Withdraw gradually	51.3%
Not sure	5.2%

(Source: Associated Television News/Zogby America Poll of 1,005 likely voters conducted 7/9/08 through 7/14/08. Margin of Error +/- 3.2 percentage points)

SPENDING

Some people think the government is trying to do too many things that should be left to individuals and businesses. Others think that government should do more to solve our country's problems. Which comes closer to your own view?

	All Americans
Government doing too much	49.0%
Obama Position ▶ Government should do more	43.0%
No Opinion	8.0%

(Gallup Poll conducted September 14-16, 2007)

WHO ARE THE AMERICANS WHO DON'T PAY TAXES?

According to poll results, of the roughly 30 percent of Americans who don't have to pay taxes, either because their income level is below the threshold that would require them to pay taxes, or because tax deductions leave them with no tax liability:

A strong majority will vote for Barack Obama.

- 60% say they will vote for Barack Obama for president.

- 31% say they will vote for John McCain for president.

- 2% say they will vote for someone else.

- 7% are not sure who they will vote for.

More than half are Democrats.

- 51% are Democrats.

- 27% are Republicans.

- 22% are Independents.

Most are between the ages of 30 and 49.

- 30% are 18-29 years of age.

- 37% are 30-49 years of age.

- 16% are 50-64 years of age.

- 17% are 65 years of age or older.

Most do not have a college degree.

- 58% do not have a college degree.

- 42% have a college degree.

A majority are not married.

- 46% are married.

- 54% are single, divorced, widowed, or separated.

A strong majority are either liberal or moderate in their political views.

- 30% are self-described Liberals or Progressives.

- 31% are self-described Moderates.

- 38% are self-described Conservatives.

- Less than 1% are self-described Libertarians.

More than half do not attend church once per week.

- 29% rarely or never attend church.

- 3% attend church only on holidays.

- 20% attend church once or twice a month.

- 33% attend church once a week.

- 16% attend church more than once a week.

More than half have an annual income of less than $50,000.

- 60% have an annual income of less than $50,000.

- 34% have an annual income between $50,000 and $100,000.

- 6% have an annual income of more than $100,000.

(Source: Associated Television News/Zogby America Poll of 1,005 likely voters conducted 7/9/08 through 7/14/08. Margin of Error +/- 3.2 percentage points)

POTENTIAL SOLUTIONS

We asked two additional questions to determine how Americans viewed potential solutions to current problems. The first deals with the problem of illegal immigrants. The second addresses the strain that retiring Baby Boomers, or even the wealthy, are placing on Social Security, and offers a solution where talented executives might come from to fill jobs when Baby Boomers retire. Please note that no one running for president has a position on these solutions, and they are not currently being debated in Congress.

The U.S. Government issues 55,000 Green Cards every year through the Diversity Immigrant Visa Program, commonly known as the Green Card Lottery. Applicants are selected randomly by a computer-generated drawing. If selected, the main applicant, spouse and all unmarried children under twenty-one years of age will have a chance to apply for permanent resident status in the United States. Illegal immigrants are currently ineligible to register for the green card lottery.

Would you support or oppose a government plan for a similar lottery for illegal immigrants as a way to induce them to register with the government and pay a fine? Illegal immigrants who register would still have a chance to become a U.S citizen. Those who don't register would be permanently denied an opportunity to become a U.S citizen.

	All Americans	Democratic	Republican	Independent
Support	57.8	60.9	49.5	64.6
Oppose	36.6	33.0	44.1	31.5
NS	5.6	6.1	6.4	3.9
Total	100.0	100.0	100.0	100.0

(Source: Associated Television News/Zogby America Poll of 1,005 likely voters conducted 7/9/08 through 7/14/08. Margin of Error +/- 3.2 percentage points)

Given the strain the aging Baby boomers will put on Social Security would you favor or oppose allowing people over sixty-five to defer drawing Social Security for a few additional years while they remain in the work force? Earnings at age sixty-five and over would be taxed at the lower capital gains rate instead of the ordinary income rate.

	All Americans	70% who pay taxes	30% who don't pay taxes
Favor	77.2	78.9	72.9
Oppose	16.4	14.7	20.9

(Source: Associated Television News/Zogby America Poll of 1,005 likely voters conducted 7/9/08 through 7/14/08. Margin of Error +/- 3.2 percentage points)

For new, breaking information on Barack Obama since this book was published, please go to www.audacityofdeceit.com. If you have friends who would like to receive this chapter, or any of the chapters in this book, please refer them to the same Web site where they can download the chapter of their choice for free.

CHAPTER TWELVE

TRUST

"Barack Obama went out of his way to create the impression that he was a new kind of political leader more honest, less cynical and less relentlessly calculating than most... Obama is not just tacking gently toward the center. He's lurching right when it suits him, and he's zigging with the kind of reckless abandon that's guaranteed to cause disillusion, if not whiplash."[1]

—*New York Times* Columnist Bob Herbert

O NCE, at a dinner function, I introduced a staff member of mine to President Reagan. When he saw she was attractive and found out that her name was Molly Malone, he immediately displayed warmth and humor, on the verge of singing the Irish song by the same name. He stopped himself, however, and told us he'd probably be singing that song to himself all night.

I worked for Ronald Reagan when he ran against Gerald Ford and did over fifteen major fundraisers with him when he was governor of California and, later, when he was president. Filled with his humor, my award-winning video on President Reagan couldn't have been made without his personal help.

Comparing Ronald Reagan to Barack Obama, Obama seems humorless. Obama doesn't express the same kind of personal warmth that Reagan exuded, but measures every word, plans every gesture. When he deviates from this script, he creates doubt. As Obama formulates his positions, we Americans hear three different responses: yesterday's response, today's response, tomorrow's response. Thus, the would-be president is completely incapable of, and unwilling to, debate his presidential rival in "town-hall" meetings, where he won't be able to anticipate the questions, plan the gestures, nor carefully script his words.

Is there a problem with a candidate who changes his position on almost every single issue, solely to improve his chances of winning the presidential election? Probably not, except:

- *If Barack Obama held these positions in January 2008, it's clear that he would not have won the primary battles against Hillary Clinton, who would have been the Democratic nominee;*

- *If the voters who secured the nomination for him cannot trust Obama to keep his word, can the rest of us trust him to keep his word after November?*

The fact is, Obama has effortlessly changed his position on an entire range of issues facing all of the presidential candidates. Consider:

- FISA: In October, the Obama campaign pledged he would filibuster "any bill that includes retroactive immunity for telecommunications companies." According to Obama spokesman Bill Burton, "To be clear: Barack will support a filibuster of any bill that includes retroactive immunity for telecommunications companies."[2] "[T]he presumptive Democratic nominee has angered some of his most ardent supporters while triggering something of an online mutiny. Thousands are using MyBarackObama.com to angrily organize against him because of a changed position on terrorist wiretap legislation…"[3]

- Public Financing: In September 2007, asked if he would agree to public financing of the presidential election if his GOP opponent did the same, Obama replied "yes." Obama later attached several conditions to such an agreement, including regulating spending by outside groups and his spokesman argued the candidate never committed himself on the matter.[4]

- Gun Control: After the Supreme Court overturned the District of Columbia's gun ban, the gun ban extremist now says he favors both an individual's right to own a gun as well as the government's right to regulate ownership.[5]

- Hunting: Obama's campaign Web site states: "Barack Obama did not grow up hunting and fishing, but he recognizes the great conservation legacy of America's hunters and anglers and has great respect for the passion that hunters and anglers have for their sport."[6] But in 2005, Obama voted to ban almost all center-fire rifle ammunition commonly used for hunting and sport shooting.[7]

- Faith-based Initiatives: On the campaign trail, Senator Obama planned to slam President Bush's faith-based program as "a photo op" and a failure, saying he would scrap the office and create a new Council for Faith-Based and Neighborhood Partnerships that would be a "critical" part of his administration.[8] Yet, the very same day, Obama reached out to evangelical voters, announcing plans to expand President Bush's program steering federal social service dollars to religious groups and—in a move sure to cause controversy—support their ability to hire and fire based on faith.[9]

- Gay Marriage: "I still think that these are decisions that need to be made at a state and local level,"

Obama told ABC News on June 16, 2008. "I'm a strong supporter of civil unions. And I think that, you know, we're involved in a national conversation about this issue."[10] Two weeks later, on July 1, 2008, Obama told a San Francisco-based Lesbian Gay Bisexual Transgender group that he opposes a California ballot measure that would ban same-sex marriage.[11]

• Iran: ABC World News reported Senator Barack Obama's reaction to Iranian missile tests in July 2008. "The United States has to gather up others in the region, as well as internationally, to apply pressure on Iran," Obama said. "But it's very difficult for us to do so when we haven't shown a willingness to engage in the sort of direct negotiations with Iran that would give them carrots and sticks for a change in behavior." Then, the CBS Evening News reported that Obama said the situation called for direct diplomacy and the threat of tougher sanctions to persuade Iran to drop its nuclear program.[12]

• Iraq: Obama said that a Democratic administration would not take any irresponsible, reckless, sudden decisions or action to endanger our gains, our achievements, our stability, or our security, but that he would reach any decision through close consultation with the Iraqi government and U.S. military commanders in the field.[13] In April 2008, Obama said, "I will listen to General Petraeus given the experience that he has accumulated over the last several years. It would be stupid of me to ignore what he has to say." Obama added, "But it is my job as president; it would be my job as commander-in-chief, to set the mission…[14]

- Welfare Reform: Aligning himself late in the game with welfare reform, Obama launched a television ad which touts the way the overhaul "slashed the rolls by 80 percent." Obama leaves out, however, that he was against the 1996 federal legislation that precipitated the caseload reduction. "I am not a defender of the status quo with respect to welfare," Obama said on the floor of the Illinois State Senate on May 31, 1997. "Having said that, I probably would not have supported the federal legislation, because I think it had some problems."[15]

- NAFTA: In October 2007, Obama announced he would vote for a Peruvian trade agreement that would expand NAFTA to that country. In fact, while he was the first presidential candidate to declare support for the NAFTA expansion, Obama also said he opposed NAFTA from the start and U.S. workers were not the only ones to suffer from its effects. Wages and benefits in Mexico had not been improved by the treaty, he said.[16]

- Special Interests: In January 2008, the Obama campaign decried union contributions to Hillary Clinton's and John Edwards's campaigns as "special interest" money. Obama changed his tune as he began gathering his own union endorsements. He now respectfully refers to unions as the representatives of "working people" and says he is "thrilled" by their support.[17]

- The Cuba Embargo: In January 2004, Obama said it was time "to end the embargo with Cuba" because it had "utterly failed in the effort to overthrow Castro. But, speaking to a Cuban American audience in Miami in August

2007, Obama said he would not "take off the embargo" as president because it is "an important inducement for change."[18]

- Illegal Immigration: In a March 2004 questionnaire, Obama was asked if the government should crack down on businesses that hire illegal immigrants. He replied "Oppose." But in a presidential primary debate televised in January 2008, he said that we do have to crack down on those employers that are taking advantage of the situation.[19]

- Decriminalization of Marijuana: Running for the U.S. Senate in January 2004, Obama told Illinois college students that he supported eliminating criminal penalties for marijuana use. But in an early presidential primary debate in October 2007, he joined other Democratic candidates in opposing the decriminalization of marijuana.[20]

This is a pretty dismal record, even more so when we reflect, again, on Ronald Reagan's presidency. Many voters who supported him did so even if they disagreed with his positions. Why? They supported him because they believed he was a man true to his word, a man who didn't change for the sake of political convenience. *A new kind of politician*, Ronald Reagan held to his views.

We might have thought Barack Obama was this kind of man, a steadfast leader, true to his vision. After all, he said he was a new kind of politician.

But Obama's flip-flops are the calculated maneuverings of a candidate willing to say anything to get elected. In fact, his history of re-inventing himself suggests a life-long pattern of deceit:

OBAMA REWRITE: "But something stirred across the country because of what happened in Selma, Alabama, because some folks were willing to march across a bridge.... So they got together, Barack Obama, Jr. was born... So don't tell me I don't have a claim on Selma, Alabama."[21]

REALITY: Born on August 4, 1961, Barack Obama's birth was not influenced by the Selma march, which took place in 1965, a year after his mother filed for divorce.[22]

OBAMA REWRITE: "Present" votes are common in Illinois.

REALITY: Not many, if any, state legislators have 130 "present" votes.

OBAMA REWRITE: I was a professor of law.

REALITY: A senior lecturer with the University of Chicago, Obama technically considers himself to be a professor but he is not a full-time "professor" nor is he on tenure track.[23]

Some might argue that flip-flops are mere policy tweaks, nothing more than splitting hairs but, in sum, they create a smokescreen for Obama's troubling pattern of concealment and deceit. His relationships with radical leftists are probably the best example of Obama's concealment. In what might well be Obama's best prestidigitation, he misdirected the media into focusing only on his political career and, in the process, gave himself a free pass on the discussion of his lengthy history of connections to radical leftists.

FRIENDS OF OBAMA

Until recently, America thought that Obama's only radical link (other than Reverend Jeremiah Wright) was the "guy who lived in his neighborhood," or, as we now know him, Bill Ayers. But thanks to the work of some inquisitive reporters and bloggers, we also know that Obama's earliest introduction to socialism and socialists was during his childhood. And this is the greatest secret Obama has kept from the voters: his lifelong association with socialism. "This is as openly radical a background as any significant American political figure has ever emerged from, as much Malcolm X as Martin Luther King Jr.," wrote Ben Wallace-Wells of Barack Obama for *Rolling Stone* in February 2007.[24]

As an adult, Obama's connections to radical leftists grew to include unabashed former terrorists Bill Ayers and Bernadine Dohrn, Marxist Cornel West, Maoist Carl Davidson, as well as several activist flavors in between.[25] Obama deftly glosses over this part of his past in nearly every biographical profile he provides. But these connections explain the presence of these individuals in and around his campaign and reveal why, for instance, Obama's official campaign Web site features a "Marxists/ Socialists/Communists for Obama" community blog (although the Obama campaign adds that such groups do not represent the viewpoints of the campaign).[26] These individuals and their organizations warrant closer inspection.

THE AYERS FAMILY TREE

Thomas Ayers

President and CEO of Commonwealth Edison from 1973 to 1980, Thomas Ayers was a lifelong liberal and a prominent Chicago businessman. Tom Ayers served on the boards of G.D. Searle, Chicago Pacific Corporation, Zenith Corporation, Northwest Industries, First National Bank of Chicago, and the Tribune Company (which owned the *Chicago Tribune*), and worked with many nonprofit organizations including Chicago United, Community Renewal Society, the Chicago Community Trust, the Chicago Chamber of Commerce, and the Chicago Urban League. These philanthropic organizations drive politics in Illinois, and Tom Ayers was a very powerful political figure in Chicago. He was also the father of Bill Ayers and his brother John.

The common thread between Obama and the jobs he held before he began his political career, Thomas Ayers and his family are bound by many strong connections to Obama:

Developing Communities Project

Santa Clara University School of Law Professor Steve Diamond speculates that Obama first became acquainted with Tom and Bill Ayers during his earlier effort with the Developing Communities Project (DCP). Obama's DCP, which originated in the radical movement started by veteran Chicago organizer Saul Alinsky, worked alongside a broad-based school reform coalition headed by Tom Ayers in 1987. Diamond speculates that Tom Ayers most likely knew Obama even before he left Chicago for Harvard Law School.

Sidley Austin

Tom Ayers served on the board of trustees of Northwestern University alongside Commonwealth Edison's long-time outside counsel, Howard Trienens (a senior partner at the law firm of Sidley Austin), and Newton Minnow (another Sidley Austin partner). During his first year of law school, Obama was a summer intern with Sidley Austin in Chicago.

Leadership Council of Chicago Public Schools

Tom and John Ayers served together with Obama on the Leadership Council of the Chicago Public Schools Education fund in 2001 and 2002.

Chicago Transit Board

Unpaid senior campaign adviser and Obama confidant Valerie Jarrett was formerly the chairperson of the Chicago Transit Board, which Tom Ayers helped to create.

Ask Strategies

When Commonwealth Edison wanted state lawmakers to back a hefty rate increase, they employed Ask Strategies, which devised a bogus entity to advocate rate hikes through a series of ads designed to get customers to favor the rate hike. The president of Ask Strategies is none other than David Axelrod, Obama's top campaign adviser and strategist in 2008.

Community Renewal Society

Tom Ayers played a role in funding organizations for which Obama worked. For example, Tom Ayers sat on a number of boards, including the Community Renewal Society, which Diamond notes funds projects for Reverend Jeremiah Wright's Trinity United Church of Christ.

The Gamaliel Foundation

Obama also worked at The Gamaliel Foundation, which teaches the works and practices of Saul Alinsky to community organizers. The Gamaliel Foundation is a church-based foundation, which is supported by many of Tom Ayers foundations. It also happens to be a part of the United Church of Christ and associated with Reverend Wright.[27]

Northern Trust

Tom Ayers is also linked to Northern Trust, the bank that holds Obama's mortgage. Before he retired in 1994, Ayers served on the Finance Committee of the General Dynamics Corporation board of directors. Northern Trust was the trustee of the corporation's Salaried Savings Plan and the Hourly Savings Plan that was overseen by the committee.

Woods Fund

Tom Ayer's son William served on the board of the Woods Fund with Obama. As board members, William "Bill" Ayers and Obama helped direct grant money from the Foundation. Among the recipients were two of Tom Ayers's pet organizations: The Chicago Urban League ($50,000 grant) and the Chicago Public Education Fund ($100,000).

Bill Ayers

After college, Obama headed to Chicago, the stomping ground of an earlier influence in his life, Frank Marshall Davis, who happened to be a member of the Communist Party USA. In Chicago, Obama eventually met Bill Ayers, a former Weather Undergound member, domestic terrorist, and socialist. Of all the radical leftists in the Obama camp, none has received more ink than Bill Ayers and his wife Bernadine Dohrn, perhaps because both are unrepentant former members of the 1960s-era terrorist organization, the Weather Underground. Ironically, on Sept. 11, 2001, The *New York Times* ran a story about Ayers, quoting him saying, "I don't regret setting bombs. I feel we didn't do enough."[28]

Law Professor Steve Diamond speculates that Obama could have met Ayers as early as 1986 to 1988, before he left for Harvard Law School. This would completely dispel Obama's claim that Ayers was "just a guy who lived in my neighborhood."

The Weather Underground was an offshoot of Students for a Democratic Society, a student activist movement consisting of socialists, Marxists and Maoists. This group was behind the riots at the 1968 Democratic National Convention. The following year, the organization splintered and fell apart, but not before giving birth to the Weather Underground, a domestic terror group involved in the bombing of the U.S. Capitol in 1971 and the Pentagon in 1972.

Obama's connection to Ayers came under the national spotlight during the April 16, 2008, Democratic presidential candidate debate, when moderator George Stephanopoulos approached the subject of Obama and Ayers.

"A gentleman named William Ayers, he was part of the Weather Underground in the 1970s," Stephanopoulos started. "They bombed the Pentagon, the Capitol, and other buildings. He's never apologized for that. And in fact, on 9/11 he was quoted in The *New York Times* saying, 'I don't regret setting bombs; I feel we didn't do enough.' An early organizing meeting for your state senate campaign was held at his house, and your campaign has said you are friendly," Stephanopoulos continued.

"Can you explain that relationship for the voters, and explain to Democrats why it won't be a problem?"

"George, but this is an example of what I'm talking about," Obama replied. "This is a guy who lives in my neighborhood, who's a professor of English in Chicago, who I know and who I have not received some official endorsement from. He's not somebody who I exchange ideas from on a regular basis. And the notion that somehow as a consequence of me knowing somebody who engaged in detestable acts forty years ago when I was eight years old, somehow reflects on me and my values, doesn't make much sense, George."[29]

But, thanks to some brilliant legwork by professor and political scientist Steve Diamond, we have a more complete understanding of the Ayers-Obama relationship. And the facts don't point to Mr. Obama's neighborhood.

Alliance for Better Schools

Bill Ayers, Anne C. Hallett, and Warren Chapman of the Joyce Foundation (of which Obama is a board member) sat down in December 1993 to begin work on a proposal to the Annenberg Challenge for support of Chicago's public school reform efforts. The effort, of which Ayers was very proud, established

Local School Councils (LSC) in the wake of the 1987 teachers' strike. The Alliance for Better Schools (ABCs) was then formed to push for the LSC idea in the Illinois state legislature. In addition to Ayers, other active players in the ABCs were:

- Barack Obama's Developing Communities Project;

- Chicago United, a group of businessmen concerned about race and education issues, which was founded by Bill Ayers' father, Tom Ayers.[30]

The Annenberg Challenge

The Annenberg Challenge, a foundation created by a $500 million gift by philanthropist Walter H. Annenberg, awarded the City of Chicago a $49.2 million grant based on Ayers' proposal that was, in effect, an attempt to rescue the LSC concept, which was in danger of falling to a re-centralization effort. In 1995, the award gave birth to the Chicago Annenberg Challenge (CAC), which had three overlapping entities: The Chicago Annenberg Challenge Board (the Board); the Chicago School Reform Collaborative (the Collaborative); and the Consortium of Chicago Schools Research (CCSR). The first chairman of the CAC Board was a third-year associate at the law firm of Davis, Miner, Barnhill & Galland, a thirty-three-year-old lawyer named Barack Obama. He initiated the board position in early 1995 and stepped down in late 1999.[31] During the intervening four years, Obama was the principal in charge of executing the mission laid out in Bill Ayers' CAC proposal.

Chicago School Reform Collaborative

Bill Ayers headed the second overlapping entity of the CAC, the Chicago School Reform Collaborative.[32]

Hugo Chavez

The LSCs look "eerily similar to efforts by regimes like those in Nicaragua under the Sandinistas and Venezuela under [Hugo] Chavez to impose control over teachers and their independent unions by an authoritarian regime," notes law professor Steve Diamond. "Thus it is not a surprise to me that Bill Ayers has traveled several times in recent years to Venezuela where he has spoken in front of Hugo Chavez and has enthusiastically applauded the regime's efforts to link education policy to the Chavez revolution."[33]

Joyce Foundation

By the time Obama stepped down from the CAC Board in 1999, it had collected approximately $60 million, including $11 million from the Joyce Foundation (on whose board Obama sat from 1998 until 2001) and $1 million from the Woods Fund (on whose board Obama was a director from 1999 until December 11, 2002).[34] Tom Ayers was a silent influence behind several of the organizations that made grants to the CAC.

Ayers and Obama Served as Co-panelists

Bill Ayers also served as a panelist with Barack Obama on two occasions. On November 20, 1997, Obama joined Bill Ayers and two other panelists for a University of Chicago-sponsored panel that debated the merits of the juvenile justice system. The panel was put together by none other than Obama's wife, Michelle, who was Associate Dean of Student Services at the school.[35] On April 20, 2002, Obama again served on a panel with Bill Ayers, sponsored by The Center for Public Intellectuals and the University of Illinois-Chicago.[36]

Ayers Hosted Obama Campaign Event

Finally, Ayers and his wife, Bernadine, hosted a meet-and-greet at their house to introduce Obama to their neighbors during his first run for the Illinois Senate. Ayers contributed $200 to Obama's campaign in 2001.[37]

Bernadine Dohrn

An Associate Professor of Law at Northwestern University, Bernardine Dohrn is the wife of Bill Ayers. Like her husband, she was involved in Students for a Democratic Society (SDS) and the Weather Underground and, also like her husband, she spent much of the 1970s eluding the FBI, for Ayers and Dohrn were both on their "Ten Most Wanted List" for the string of bombings they committed in the U.S. In 1980 she and her husband surrendered to authorities and all charges against them were dropped on the grounds that the fugitives were illegally surveilled. Dohrn pled guilty, however, to charges of aggravated battery and bail jumping, for which she received probation. She later served less than a year in prison for refusing to testify in the trial of former Weatherman Susan Rosenberg.

In addition to the meet-and-greet that Dohrn and Bill Ayers hosted for Obama during his first run for the Illinois Senate, Obama shares additional connections with Dohrn. They both worked at Sidley Austin, outside counsel for Thomas Ayers' company, Commonwealth Edison. Sidley hired Dohrn despite the fact that she had no law degree. A senior partner later allowed that they hired her as a personal favor, but didn't say to whom (but most likely Tom Ayers). How difficult would it have been to get a law student hired at Sidley Austin using the same connections?

Remember the 2008 primary debate, when Stephanopoulos asked presidential candidate Obama about his relationship with the former domestic terrorist. Obama claimed Ayers was a "guy in my neighborhood... when I was eight years old" and "not somebody who I exchange ideas from on a regular basis," and that the relationship shouldn't "reflect on me and my values." Obviously, Obama deceived the American people with these claims. Obviously he knew Bill Ayers: Both were active in the Alliance for Better Schools; Obama worked to carry out Ayers' mission with the Chicago Annenberg Challenge; both shared leadership roles and involvement in various foundations; both shared panels at speaking events; and Bill Ayers and Bernadine Dohrn hosted a campaign event for Obama *in their home.*

FRIENDS OF AYERS AND OBAMA

Michael Klonsky

Until June 2008, Michael Klonsky had a blog that covered education politics and teaching for social justice on Obama's official presidential campaign Web site. After journalists and bloggers began to reveal Klonsky's past, the blog was airbrushed out of existence. So who is Michael Klonsky?

Obama and his campaign don't want us to know that Klonsky is also a friend of Bill Ayers. In fact, Klonsky belonged to the radical '60s organization Students for a Democratic Society, which gave birth to the Weather Underground. On May 12, 1969, Klonsky and four other SDSers were arrested at the organization's Chicago national headquarters for assaulting a police officer, interfering with a firefighter, and inciting mob action.[38] According to Professor Steve Diamond:

> Klonsky was one of the most destructive hardline maoists in the [Students for a Democratic Society] SDS in the late 60s who emerged from SDS to form a pro-Chinese sect called the October League that later became the Beijing-recognized Communist Party (Marxist-Leninist). As chairman of the party, Klonsky traveled to Beijing itself in 1977 and, literally, toasted the Chinese Stalinist leadership who, in turn, "hailed the formation of the CP(ML) as 'reflecting the aspirations of the

proletariat and working people,' effectively recognizing the group as the all-but-official U.S. Maoist party."[39]

Carl Davidson

Carl Davidson is an American Marxist who serves as a national steering committee member of United for Peace and Justice, a field organizer for the Solidarity Economy Network, and co-chair of Chicagoans Against War & Injustice. A key organizer for Obama's 2002 anti-war demonstration hosted by Chicagoans Against War & Injustice, Davidson has known Obama since 1996, when the candidate came to him to discuss an endorsement by the New Party. Davidson was a major player in the Chicago branch of the New Party, a Marxist political coalition whose objective was to endorse and elect leftist public officials. In other words, Obama sought (and received) the endorsement of a Marxist political coalition for his state Senate race in 1996.

FrontPage Magazine's DiscoverTheNetworks, a Web site dedicated to profiling the political left, described Davidson. "As a college student in the 1960s, Davidson was a national secretary of Students of a Democratic Society and a national leader of the anti-Vietnam War movement. He received a bachelor's degree in philosophy from Penn State University and later found employment as a philosophy instructor at the University of Nebraska, also in the 1960s." *FrontPage* further reported that "Davidson and Tom Hayden take credit for having launched in 1969 the "Venceremos Brigades," which covertly transported hundreds of young Americans to Cuba to help harvest sugar cane and interact with Havana's communist revolutionary leadership. (The Brigades were organized by Fidel Castro's Cuban intelligence agency, which trained '*brigadistas*' in guerrilla warfare techniques, including the use of arms and explosives.)"[40]

Davidson is also a member of Progressives for Obama, an organization founded by actors Danny Glover, Tom Hayden, and others.

Marilyn Katz

Marilyn Katz is head of the public relations firm, MK Communications, and an "Obama bundler" who agreed to raise at least $50,000 each for the campaign.[41] In fact, the blog site Rezko Watch states that she and her husband committed to raising $200,000 for Obama.[42] Katz also helped organize, alongside her friend and fellow former SDS member Carl Davidson, the October 2, 2002, anti-war protest sponsored by Chicagoans Against War and Injustice, where Obama spoke against the war in Iraq.[43]

According to the *Chicago Sun-Times*, "Katz met Ayers when he was seventeen and they were members of Students for a Democratic Society, a peaceful group from which the Weather Underground splintered."[44] Katz oversaw security for the SDS and was at the 1968 Chicago Convention and at the eye of the protests that took place that year.[45]

Tom Hayden

Jane Fonda-ex and SDS founder Tom Hayden is one of the founders of Progressives for Obama.[46] On January 28, 2008, he endorsed Obama for president.[47]

FrontPage's DiscoverTheNetworks.org described Hayden:

> As a young man, Tom Hayden was a principal organizer of Students for a Democratic Society (SDS), which became the leading radical organization of its day. The then-twenty-two-year-old Hayden authored the SDS political manifesto, known as the Port Huron Statement, which the group's founding members adopted in 1962. This document condemned the American political system as the cause of international conflict

and a variety of social ills—including racism, materialism, militarism, and poverty.

Among the most visible and outspoken mouthpieces of the pro-Communist camp during the Vietnam War era, in the early 1970s Hayden organized—along with his wife Jane Fonda, John Kerry, and Ted Kennedy—an "Indo-China Peace Campaign" (IPC) to cut off American aid to the regimes in Cambodia and South Vietnam. The IPC worked tirelessly to help the North Vietnamese Communists and the Khmer Rouge (led by Pol Pot) emerged victorious.[48]

Cass Sunstein

Another Obama advisor, Sunstein is professor at the University of Chicago Law School. In 2004, Sunstein authored "The Second Bill of Rights: FDR's Unfinished Revolution and Why We Need It More Than Ever," in which he argued that rights are discretionary grants from the government to the citizen.[49]

Jodie Evans

Like Marilyn Katz, Evans is also an Obama bundler who committed to raise $50,000 for the Obama campaign. She also founded Code Pink, a feminist anti-war group dedicated to protesting the war in Iraq. This highly visible outfit protested outside Walter Reed Army Medical Center with signs that read "Maimed for Lies" and "Enlist Here and Die for Haliburton." Code Pink lined up mock caskets outside the Army hospital.[50]

More than just an anti-war protester, Evans is also a radical leftist with some pedigree. "[She]… sits on the board of directors of the Rain Forest Action Network (RAN), a coalition of anti-capitalist, anti-corporate environmentalist groups," *FrontPage* reported. "RAN's co-founder Michael Roselle also founded the Earth Liberation Front, which the FBI ranks alongside the Animal Liberation Front as the foremost domestic terrorism threats in the United States. According to the FBI, during the past seven years those two groups have been responsible for more than six hundred criminal acts and $43 million in damages...."

Evans also sits on the advisory board of the International Occupation Watch (IOW) center in Iraq, which Code Pink helped establish. Occupation Watch organizers Medea Benjamin and Leslie Cagan explicitly declared their purpose in setting up headquarters in Baghdad was to "thin U.S. forces by getting soldiers to declare themselves conscientious objectors."[51]

Evans is also notorious for making ridiculous and insensitive remarks. For example, during a radio interview with Paul Ibbetson on his "Conscience of Kansas" radio show, Ibbetson tried to explain that the U.S. hadn't done anything to provoke the 9/11 attacks. Evans replied that we were in Saudi Arabia, which she claimed was reason enough for al-Qaeda and Osama bin Laden to kill thousands of Americans in terrorist attacks. While Evans said, "I don't think any terrorist attack is justified," she added that we should listen to Osama bin Laden and change our policies because "Sometimes, it would be a good idea to listen to why someone is trying to blow you up."[52]

Obama's history with this *cabal* of radicals explains his liberal record in the Illinois State Senate and the U.S. Senate. Psychiatrist Dr. Lyle Rossiter, author of *The Liberal Mind*, analyzed this mind-set and described the values that embody Obama and his campaign:

> What the liberal mind is passionate about is a world filled with pity, sorrow, neediness, misfortune, poverty, suspicion, mistrust, anger, exploitation, discrimination, victimization, alienation, and injustice. Those who occupy this world are "workers," "minorities," "the little guy," "women," and the "unemployed." They are poor, weak, sick, wronged, cheated, oppressed, disenfranchised, exploited, and victimized. They bear no responsibility for their problems. None of their agonies are attributable to faults or failings of their own: not to poor choices,

bad habits, faulty judgment, wishful thinking, lack of ambition, low frustration tolerance, mental illness, or defects in character. None of the victims' plight is caused by failure to plan for the future or learn from experience. Instead, the "root causes" of all this pain lie in faulty social conditions: poverty, disease, war, ignorance, unemployment, racial prejudice, ethnic and gender discrimination, modern technology, capitalism, globalization and imperialism. In the radical liberal mind, this suffering is inflicted on the innocent by various predators and persecutors: "Big Business," "Big Corporations," "greedy capitalists," U.S. Imperialists," "the oppressors," "the rich," "the wealthy," "the powerful" and "the selfish."

As is the case in all personality disturbance, defects of this type represent serious failures in development processes. The nature of these failures is detailed below. Among their consequences are the liberal mind's relentless efforts to misrepresent human nature and to deny certain indispensable requirements for human relating. In his efforts to construct a grand collectivist utopia—to live what Jacques Barzun has called "the unconditioned life" in which "everybody should be safe and at ease in a hundred ways"—the radical liberal attempts to actualize in the real world an idealized fiction that will mitigate all hardship and heal all wounds. (Barzun 2000). He acts out this fiction, essentially a Marxist morality play, in various theaters of human relatedness, most often on the world's economic, social, and political stages. But the play repeatedly folds. Over the course of the twentieth century, the radical liberal's attempts to create a brave new socialist world have invariably failed. At the dawn of the twenty-first century his attempts continue to fail in the stagnant economies, moral decay and social turmoil now widespread in Europe. An increasingly bankrupt welfare society is putting the U.S. on track for the same fate if liberalism is not cured there. Because the liberal agenda's principles violate the rules of ordered liberty, his most determined efforts to realize its visionary fantasies must inevitably fall short. Yet, despite all the evidence against it, the modern liberal mind believes his agenda is good social science. It is, in fact, bad science fiction. He persists in this agenda despite its madness.[53]

ENTITIES RELEVANT TO THE AYERS-OBAMA CONNECTION

Developing Communities Project

Barack Obama's first job out of college was with the Developing Communities Project, a church-based community organization. Obama's job was funded through a $25,000 grant from the Woods Fund. The DCP worked alongside organizations in which Tom Ayers was active in promoting education reform in Chicago. Obama noted in *Dreams from My Father* that the DCP had its origins in the radical movement started by Chicago organizer and socialist, Saul Alinsky, who also was a friend of Tom Ayers.

Woods Fund

According to *FrontPage* magazine, "The Woods Fund of Chicago is an outgrowth of the Woods Charitable Fund (WCF), which was established in 1941 by Frank Woods and his wife, Nelle Cochrane Woods. Frank Woods was an attorney and a nationally prominent telephone company executive.... The Fund focused on welfare reform, affordable housing, the quality of public schools, race and class disparities in the juvenile justice system, and tax policy as a tool in reducing poverty. The Fund supported the concept of an expanding welfare state allocating ever-increasing amounts of money to the public school system, and the redistribution of wealth via taxes."[54]

Obama served on the Woods Fund Board from 1993 to 2002. In 1999, Bill Ayers joined the board and served alongside Obama for three years. The board met quarterly, so Obama and Ayers had at least a dozen opportunities to get to know each other (if they hadn't already done so). In 2001, Woods Fund board chairman Howard J. Stanback headed New Kenwood LLC, a limited liability company founded by Tony Rezko and Obama's former law firm boss, Allison Davis. In

1987, the Woods Fund made a $36,000 grant to Obama's DCP for school reform work and in 2001, they gave a $6,000 grant to Rev. Jeremiah Wright's Trinity United Church of Christ.

Between 2001 and 2002, when Obama was director of the board, the Woods Fund gave a total of $75,000 to the Arab American Action Network (AAAN), an anti-Israel outfit run by Mona Khalidi.[55] Mona is the wife of Rashid Khalidi, and both are friends of Obama's from his days at the University of Chicago. A University of Chicago professor who was interviewed for this book, speaking on the condition of anonymity, said the relationship between Khalidi and Obama was so close that the Obamas used to babysit the Khalidis' children.

According to journalist Aaron Klein, there's more. "AAAN co-founder Rashid Khalidi was reportedly a director of the official PLO [Palestine Liberation Organization] press agency WAFA in Beirut from 1976 to 1982," Klein reported, "while the PLO committed scores of anti-Western attacks and was labeled by the U.S. as a terror group. Khalidi's wife, AAAN President Mona Khalidi, was reportedly WAFA's English translator during that period."[56]

During documented speeches and public events, Rashid Khalidi has called Israel an "apartheid system in creation" and a destructive "racist" state.[57]

When Khalidi departed the University of Chicago in 2003, Obama delivered an in-person testimonial at a farewell ceremony, reminiscing about conversations over meals prepared by Mona Khalidi.[58] According to a *Los Angeles Times* account, Obama said his many talks with the Khalidis served as "consistent reminders to me of my own blind spots and my own biases…. It's for that reason that I'm hoping that, for many years to come, we continue that conversation—a conversation that is necessary not just around Mona and Rashid's dinner table," but around "this entire world."[59]

Rashid Khalidi has repeatedly suggested his support for Palestinian terror, calling Palestinian suicide bombings a response to "Israeli aggression." He dedicated his 1986 book, *Under Siege*, to "those who gave their lives...in defense of the cause of Palestine and independence of Lebanon." Critics assailed the book as excusing Palestinian terrorism.

Yet Obama, questioned about Khalidi during a 2008 campaign stop at a Boca Raton synagogue, minimized his relationship with the controversial Columbia professor. "You mentioned Rashid Khalidi, who's a professor at Columbia," said the presidential candidate. "I do know him, because I taught at the University of Chicago. And he is Palestinian. And I do know him, and I have had conversations. He is not one of my advisers; he's not one of my foreign policy people. His kids went to the Lab school where my kids go as well. He is a respected scholar, although he vehemently disagrees with a lot of Israel's policy."

The American public needs to know what other groups and notorious characters Obama and the Woods Fund supported with financial and other support, during his tenure on the board.

Gamaliel Foundation

The Gamaliel Foundation is a network of grassroots, interfaith, interracial, multi-issue organizations working together to create a more just and more democratic society. This Foundation was also organized in the tradition of Bill Ayer's friend, Saul Alinsky. Obama worked as a consultant and instructor for the Foundation during the 1980s.

Chicago Annenberg Challenge (CAC)

The Annenberg Challenge, a foundation created by a $500 million gift by philanthropist Walter H. Annenberg, awarded the City of Chicago a $49.2 million grant based on a proposal by Bill Ayers. In 1995, the thirty-three-year-old Obama was selected as the first chairman of the board for the CAC, and he served in that capacity until late 1999. During that time, Obama most likely would have worked on a daily or weekly basis with Bill Ayers, who authored the grant that created the CAC,. It would have been Ayers' responsibility to ensure that the CAC was operating according to the dictates of the grant.Chicago School Reform Collaborative (The Collaborative)

Headed by Bill Ayers, the Collaborative was an entity of the CAC.[60] In this capacity, Ayers would have had even more opportunity to interface with Barack Obama.

Chicago Public Schools Education Fund's Leadership Council

The Chicago Public Schools Education Fund succeeded the CAC. The Fund's Leadership Council is a group of more than fifty senior-level executives and Chicago civic leaders who are committed to improving school leadership and student achievement in our public schools. In 2001 and 2002, Tom and John Ayers jointly served with Obama on The Leadership Council. Northern Trust

While this bank is most commonly associated with Tony Rezko and Barack Obama, its worth mentioning again that this is also the bank that handled General Dynamic's investments for Tom Ayers, who sat on the company's finance committee of the board of directors. In addition, the Woods Fund, for which Obama served as a board member from 1993 to 2002, used Northern Trust for its financial services and paid the company $105,583 in fees and also participated in a Northern Trust private equity fund.[61]

Also, one of Obama's major campaign contributors, Susan Crown, sits on the Northern Trust board.[62]

CHICAGO POLITICIANS AND FRIENDS

Tony Rezko

Barack Obama's friendship with convicted felon Tony Rezko raises a serious question about Obama's willingness to associate with those who have a questionable past with regard to taking advantage of Chicago's poor.

Syrian-born real estate magnate and Obama law client Tony Rezko knew Obama for more than seventeen years. Rezko was recently convicted on sixteen of twenty-four corruption charges for trading on his clout as a top adviser and fundraiser to Illinois Governor Rod Blagojevich. Obama would only say the convicted felon is "not the Tony Rezko I knew," as he did with another personal friend, Reverend Jeremiah Wright, whom he also disowned in similar fashion.[63] Of course, Obama also dismissed Wright as "not the person" he had known for nearly twenty years. And when the close association between Obama and Bill Ayers raised eyebrows, Ayers suddenly became just someone who happened to live in Obama's neighborhood, nothing more.

Despite Obama's claims of not knowing the crooked side of Rezko, his former alderman in Chicago, Toni Preckwinkle, suggests otherwise. "Who you take money from is a reflection of your knowledge at the time and your principles," Preckinwinkle said.[64]

The *Chicago Sun-Times* reported that "Obama has collected at least $168,308 from Rezko and his circle. Obama also has taken in an unknown amount of money from people who attended fund-raising events hosted by Rezko since the mid-1990s."[65] Also, Obama told the *Chicago Tribune* that, during his first state Senate campaign in 1995, Rezko raised $10,000 to $15,000 of the $100,000 total collected for that race, roughly 10 to 15 percent of all the funds raised.[66]

During an interview with Preckwinkle, reporter Ryan Lizza asked her: "Can you get where he [Obama] is and maintain your personal integrity?"

"Is that a question?" Preckwinkle stared at him and grimaced. "I'm going to pass on that."[67] As Lizza reports:

> Rezko was one of the people Obama consulted when he considered running to replace [state senator Alice] Palmer, and Rezko eventually raised about ten per cent of Obama's funds for that first campaign. As a state senator, Obama became an advocate of the tax-credit program. "That's an example of a smart policy," he told the *Chicago Daily Law Bulletin* in 1997. "The developers were thinking in market terms and operating under the rules of the marketplace; but at the same time, we had government supporting and subsidizing those efforts." Obama and Rezko's friendship grew stronger. They dined together regularly and even, on at least one occasion, retreated to Rezko's vacation home, in Lake Geneva, Wisconsin.[68]

Here is what is known about Rezko's Rezmar Corporation and its relationship to Obama:

1) Rezko co-founded Rezmar Co. with his partner, Daniel Mahru, to negotiate affordable housing deals. Rezmar arranged private-public partnerships with city, state and federal governments through the tax-credit program promoted by Obama. The company collected more than $100 million.[69]

2) Between 1989 and 1998, Rezko owned and operated thirty low-income projects containing a total of 1,025 apartments in Chicago's South Side, many in Obama's state Senate district.[70]

3) Obama claims to have "worked for five hours over the course of six years during which our firm [Davis Miner Barnhill] was representing, not primarily Tony Rezko..."[71] The *Chicago Sun-Times*, however, discovered that, "As a state senator,

Barack Obama wrote letters to city and state officials supporting his political patron Tony Rezko's successful bid to get more than $14 million from taxpayers to build apartments for senior citizens. The deal included $855,000 in development fees for Rezko and his partner, Allison S. Davis, Obama's former boss, according to records from the project, which was four blocks outside Obama's state Senate district."[72]

4) During the winter of 1996-1997, the residents sat in their freezing apartments at 7000-10 South Sangamon, a building owned by Rezko. The heat was shut off for over five weeks because Rezko and his business partner said they lacked the funds to have the heat turned back on.[73]

5) The *Chicago Sun-Times* reported eleven of the thirty buildings Rezmar owned and managed were in the state Senate district Obama represented during that time, and many of the thirty [buildings] ended up in foreclosure, with tenants living in squalid conditions.[74] It's a stretch to believe that none of the tenants, freezing during the winter of 1996-1997 or living in squalid conditions called their state senator, Obama, to complain. Of course, we'll never know whether any tenants did so because Obama can't provide the disposition of those records other than to suggest that they might have been thrown away. Obama told *Sun-Times* reporter Lynn Sweet, "You know I'm not certain... I didn't have the resources to ensure that all this stuff was archived in some way; it could have been thrown out."[75]

6) Every one of Rezko's properties ran into financial difficulties within six years. More than half went into foreclosure. Chicago sued Rezmar on at least a

dozen occasions because the buildings were falling apart. A city official told the *Chicago Sun-Times,* "They just didn't pay attention to the condition of the buildings."[76] (Neither did the community activist and spokesman for America's poor, State Senator Barack Obama.)

Despite Obama's promise of change, clearly he represents nothing more than politics as usual—*at best.* The Obama campaign claims that the candidate had little association with Rezmar, generating only five billable hours of work related to Rezko's business but provided no supporting documentation to the *Chicago Sun-Times.* We're just supposed to take the campaign at their word.[77]

Rezko and Obama go back to the 1990s, when Rezko offered a job to Obama, who was still at Harvard. Obama turned it down, but the two men stayed in touch following his work for the Davis law firm that represented Rezmar Corporation. The Osamas and the Rezkos continued to have dinners together and, in 2003, the Rezkos hosted a big fundraiser at their home during Obama's bid for the U.S. Senate.[78]

Things continued to get even cozier between Rezko and Obama. According to Foundation Watch:

> Obama now admits that becoming involved with Rezko when he purchased a new home in January 2005 following his election to the U.S. Senate the previous November was a "bone-headed mistake." The terms of that involvement have received widespread publicity: Senator elect Obama and Rezko toured the property together when it was already known that Rezko was under criminal investigation. Obama and his wife Michelle subsequently paid the seller $1.65 million for their new home, $300,000 below the asking price. On the same day Mrs. Rita Rezko paid the same seller the asking price of $625,000 for the adjoining 9,000-square-foot lot. In January 2006, Mrs. Rezko sold a 10 foot-by-150 foot strip of the lot to the Obamas for $104,500, and in December she sold the remainder of the property to her husband's lawyer for $575,000.[79]

On July 9, 2008, the watchdog group Judicial Watch filed separate complaints with the Federal Election Commission and the Senate Ethics Committee over Obama's acceptance of a below-market rate mortgage loan on his home in 2005.[80] The complaint alleges that the Illinois senator reportedly received a home loan of $1.32 million at a rate of 5.625 percent, although the average going rate on that day according to two different surveys was between 5.93 and 6 percent. Further, unlike loans that were reportedly available to general consumers, Obama secured this special, below-market "super super jumbo" loan without an origination fee or discount points.[81] There's more. "It appears that due to his position as a United States senator, Barack Obama received improper special treatment from Northern Trust resulting in an illicit 'gift' which has a value of almost $125,000 in interest savings," Judicial Watch wrote in its U.S. Senate ethics complaint. "Judicial Watch therefore respectfully requests a full investigation into whether the special Northern Trust mortgage received by Senator Barack Obama constitutes a gift that is prohibited by Senate ethics rules." In its FEC complaint, Judicial Watch also calls for a full investigation into whether the special mortgage is a disguised and illegal corporate campaign contribution to Senator Obama.

"Northern Trust has supported Barack Obama's political campaigns for elected office since 1990," Judicial Watch noted in the complaints. "According to the Center for Responsive Politics, cited by the *Washington Post*, Northern Trust employees have donated $71,000."

Some interesting relationships between Obama and Northern Trust have begun to surface. One connection is Susan Crown, a major Obama campaign contributor who sits on the board of Northern Trust.[82] Further, the Woods Fund of Chicago, on whose board Obama sat from 1993 to 2001, used Northern Trust for their financial services and paid the company $105,583 in fees and also participated in a Northern Trust private equity fund.

Bill Ayers' father, Tom Ayers is another Northern Trust link. Before he retired in 1994, Tom Ayers served on the Finance Committee of the General Dynamics Corporation board of directors. Northern Trust just happened to be the trustee of the corporation's Salaried Savings Plan and the Hourly Savings Plan that was overseen by the Committee.

Thus far, the American electorate has shown a disinterest in these matters. But they should care. According to *The Liberal Mind* author Dr. Rossiter:

> It appears from this list [of his associates] that Mr. Obama is quite comfortable with persons in whom anger is a prominent dynamic, or criminal impulses are overtly expressed, or both. In fact, it would not be a stretch to conclude that he is even attracted to such persons, not just comfortable with them, given his conscious choices of pastor and friends. Your average political candidate, for example would probably not count among his friends an ex-domestic terrorist or an indicted federal defendant, nor listen on Sundays to hate speech in church, nor have a wife who angrily claims she has been victimized by American society, especially if she is highly educated in two elite universities and highly paid for her work in a third. In fact, given what we know about the way the human mind works, what would be a stretch would be any claim that Mr. Obama's relationships with this many angry and/or destructive people are purely coincidental, though we can expect his supporters to make that very claim in his defense. Indeed, from a psychodynamic perspective, his tolerance of, let alone his affection for, persons who are enduringly angry almost guarantees that he has his own anger 'issues.'"[83]

PARENTAL INFLUENCE ON OBAMA'S CHILDHOOD

> "The little world of childhood with its familiar surroundings is a model of the greater world. The more intensively the family has stamped its character upon the child, the more it

will tend to feel and see its earlier miniature world again in the bigger world of adult life."

Carl Jung, *Psychological Reflections: A Jung Anthology*, 1953

Stanley Ann Dunham

In *Dreams from My Father*, Obama describes his mother as the white woman from the flatlands of Kansas. While it is true she hailed from Kansas, it is more than a little disingenuous to suggest that Obama's mother was a woman with Heartland values. *Chicago Tribune* reporter Tim Jones visited Mercer Island, Washington, where Obama's mother, Ann Dunham, lived as a teenager. Jones spoke to her classmates and found that Dunham "touted herself as an atheist," according to her best friend at Mercer High School, Maxine Box.[84]

Also, at Mercer High, young Ann Dunham was introduced to socialist thinking. According to Jones:

> In 1955, the chairman of the Mercer Island school board, John Stenhouse, testified before the House Un-American Activities Subcommittee that he had been a member of the Communist Party. At Mercer High School, two teachers—Val Foubert and Jim Wichterman—generated regular parental thunderstorms by teaching their students to challenge societal norms and question all manner of authority. Foubert, who died recently, taught English....
>
> [Wichterman] touched the societal third rail of the 1950s: He questioned the existence of God. And he didn't stop there. "I had them read *The Communist Manifesto*, and the parents went nuts," said Wichterman... "The kids started questioning things that their folks thought shouldn't be questioned—religion, politics, parental authority," said John Hunt, a classmate. "And a lot of parents didn't like that, and they tried to get them [Wichterman and Foubert] fired."
>
> The Dunhams did not join the uproar. Madelyn and Stanley shed their Methodist and Baptist upbringing and began

attending Sunday services at the East Shore Unitarian Church in nearby Bellevue.

"In the 1950s, this was sometimes known as 'the little Red church on the hill,'" said Peter Luton, the church's senior minister, referring to the effects of McCarthyism. Skepticism, the kind that Stanley embraced and passed on to his daughter, was welcomed here.[85]

"As much as a high-school student can, she'd question anything," Wichterman told the *Seattle Times*. "What's so good about democracy? What's so good about capitalism? What's wrong with communism? What's good about communism? She had what I call an inquiring mind," Wichterman concluded.[86]

But Obama's mother was only one part of the sphere of socialist thinking in which young Barack was raised.

Barack Obama, Sr.—Muslim, Bigamist, Atheist

"All of my life, I carried a single image of my father, one that I tried to take as my own," Obama wrote in *Dreams From My Father*."[87] What was that image? It was "the father of my dreams, the man in my mother's stories, full of high-blown ideals...."[88] More, Obama adds, "It was into my father's image... that I'd packed all the attributes I sought in myself." Thus, Obama assumed his father's persona and ideals, which became a driving force in his life.

Though he said little else about just what those ideals were, they have now crystallized in the form of a 1965 paper, written by the senior Obama and published in the *East African Journal*. In the paper, titled "Problems Facing Our Socialism," the elder Obama advocated the communal ownership of land and even the forced confiscation of privately controlled land. He also called for the nationalization of "European" and "Asian" owned enterprises, and advocated handing over control of these operations to the "indigenous" black population. Further, Obama wanted to increase taxes on the rich, even up to the 100 percent level, arguing that "there is no limit on taxation if the benefits derived from public services by society measures up to the cost in taxation which they have to pay." Incidentally, this concept is not totally foreign to the younger Obama, whose plan to raise taxes on the rich conceptually mimics his fathers plan.[89]

So now we know that Obama's early life was driven by a intellectually inquisitive mother and an idealized view of his absentee father, who *certainly* subscribed to socialism— whether he had the opportunity to dabble in it or not. In any case, this early environment no doubt shaped Obama's early progressive thinking.

Obama's socialist leanings were still evident when he was in college. "To avoid being mistaken for a sellout, I chose my friends carefully. The more politically active black students. The foreign students. The Chicanos. The Marxist Professors and the structural feminists and punk-rock performance poets," Obama revealed in *Dreams From My Father*. "We smoked cigarettes and wore leather jackets. At night, in the dorms, we discussed neocolonialism, Franz Fanon, Eurocentrism, and patriarchy. When we ground out our cigarettes in the hallway carpet or set our stereos so loud that the walls began to shake, we were resisting bourgeois society's stifling constraints."[90]

Childhood Muslim Influence

Perhaps this is the first time since the presidential campaign of John F. Kennedy that a nominee's religion has had such a bearing on a major political contest. Indeed, the controversy about Obama's religious life may well raise the bar, but the fact is that both his church and his faith raise a number of serious questions.

Obama insists he was never a practicing Muslim. Like so many of his assertions, however, the facts may not bear this out. Barack Hussein Obama was born on August 4, 1961, reportedly at a hospital in Hawaii, to Barack Obama Sr., a Kenyan Muslim, and Stanley Ann Dunham, an American from Wichita, Kansas, and, originally, from Mercer Island, Washington. But, as this book goes to press, a considerable debate is emerging around the authenticity of Obama's birth certificate as posted on the Web. Some bloggers feel the published birth certificate has been altered, but the Obama campaign refuses to provide the original for press verification.

Obama's parents met at the University of Hawaii, where his father was enrolled as a foreign student. When Obama was two years old, his parents separated. After divorcing Obama's father, who was a paternal Muslim bigamist, Dunham married Lolo Soetoro, an Indonesian Muslim. In 1967 the family moved to Indonesia, the world's most populous Muslim nation, and Obama attended local schools until he was ten years old.

Widely distributed media stories reported that, in January 1968, Obama was registered as a Muslim at Jakarta's Roman Catholic Franciscus Assisi Primary School under the name Barry Soetoro. Obama's stepfather, who was listed on school documents as "L Soetoro Ma," worked for the topography department of the Indonesian Army.

Indonesian Catholic schools routinely accept non-Catholic students and exempt them from studying religion. Obama's school documents, though, wrongly list him as an Indonesian citizen. After attending the Assisi Primary School, Obama was enrolled—also as a Muslim, according to documents—in the Besuki Primary School, a public school in Jakarta.

The Loatze blog, run by an American expatriate in Southeast Asia who visited the Besuki school, noted, "All Indonesian students are required to study religion at school and a young 'Barry Soetoro' being a Muslim would have been required to study Islam daily in school. He would have been taught to read and write Arabic, to recite his prayers properly, to read and recite from the Quran and to study the laws of Islam."[91]

Indeed, in Obama's autobiography, *Dreams From My Father*, he describes the public school as "a Muslim school" and acknowledges studying the Quran. "In the Muslim school," he wrote, "the teacher wrote to tell mother I made faces during Quranic studies."

The Indonesian media have been flooded with accounts of Obama's childhood Islamic studies, some describing him as a religious Muslim. Speaking to the country's *Kaltim Post*, Tine Hahiyary, who was principal of Obama's school while he was enrolled there, said she recalls he studied the Quran in Arabic. "At that time, I was not Barry's teacher but he is still in my memory" claimed Tine, who turned eighty years old in 2008. The *Kaltim Post* reported that Obama's teacher, named Hendri, died. "I remember that he studied *mengaji* (recitation of the Quran)," Tine said.[92]

Mengaji, or the act of reading the Quran with its correct Arabic punctuation, is usually taught to more religious pupils and is not known as a secular study. Also, the Indonesian daily *Banjarmasin Post* caught up with Rony Amir, an Obama classmate and Muslim, who describes Obama as "previously quite religious in Islam."[93]

The *Los Angeles Times* sent a reporter to Jakarta and interviewed Zulfin Adi, who identified himself as among Obama's closest childhood friends. Adi said the presidential candidate prayed in a mosque, something Obama's campaign claimed he never did. "We prayed but not really seriously, just following actions done by older people in the mosque. But as kids, we loved to meet our friends and went to the mosque together and played," said Adi. In response, Obama's campaign released a new statement to the *Times*, this time stating Obama "has never been a practicing Muslim."

A March 2008 *Chicago Tribune* article seems to dispute Adi's statements to the *L.A. Times*. The *Tribune* caught up with Obama's declared childhood friend, who now describes himself as only knowing Obama for a few months in 1970 when his family moved to the neighborhood. Adi said he was unsure about his recollections of Obama. But the *Tribune* found Obama did attend mosque.

"Interviews with dozens of former classmates, teachers, neighbors and friends show that Obama was not a regular practicing Muslim when he was in Indonesia," states the *Tribune* article. But it quotes the presidential candidate's former neighbors and third grade teacher, who recall that Obama "occasionally followed his stepfather to the mosque for Friday prayers."

Daniel Pipes, director of the Middle East Forum, notes that liberal blogs cited the *Tribune* article to refute claims that Obama is Muslim, but the piece actually validates that Obama was an irregularly practicing Muslim and it confirms that Obama twice attended mosque services.

As Dr. James Dobson, founder of Focus on the Family, has noted:

> There is no substitute for parental modeling of the attitudes we wish to teach. Someone once wrote, "The footsteps a child follows are most likely to be the ones his parents thought they covered up."[94]

Will American voters take Barack Obama on faith? Or will they consider what life would really be like in Obama's America? Only time will tell.

Frank Marshall Davis: Obama's Guiding Light to Chicago

Obama was just two years old when his father abandoned him, seeking his graduate degree. His mother, too, left him with caregivers so she could seek her undergraduate and master's degrees. When he was a teen, his mother again abandoned him so she could go to Indonesia to seek her Ph.D. Then, at the age of sixteen, left on his own, Barack Obama, developed the strangest of relationships in Chicago with a non-family member, a reputed communist.

The earliest of influences on the teenaged Barack Obama was Frank Marshall Davis, a member of the Communist Party USA and an apologist for the Soviet Union. In *Dreams From My Father*, Obama describes "Frank" as "pushing eighty" when he visited Obama's family in Hawaii. Davis was a poet of "some modest notoriety" and "a contemporary of Richard Wright and Langston Hughes during his years in Chicago."[95] Obama describes "Frank and his old Black Power dashiki self" advising the young man before he left for Occidental College in 1979 at the age of eighteen.[96] These passages from *Dreams From My Father* convey that Frank Marshall Davis was something akin to a surrogate dad to Obama in those days.

"How do we know 'Frank' refers to Frank Marshall Davis," wrote Elias Crim and Matthew Vadum in the June 2008 issue of *Foundation Watch*. In a 2007 speech at the dedication of a Communist Party (CP) archive, fellow traveler and historian Gerald Horne, a professor at the University of North Carolina at Chapel Hill, clarified the relationship between Obama and Davis.

> In any case, deploring these convictions in Hawaii was an African-American poet and journalist by the name of Frank Marshall Davis, who was certainly in the orbit of the CP—if not a member—and who was born in Kansas and spent a good deal of his adult life in Chicago, before decamping to Honolulu in 1948 at the suggestion of his good friend Paul Robeson. Eventually, he befriended another family—a Euro-American family—that had migrated to Honolulu from Kansas [actually Seattle, Washington] and a young woman from this family eventually had a child with a young student from Kenya East Africa who goes by the name of Barack Obama, who retracing the steps of Davis eventually decamped to Chicago. In his best-selling memoir *Dreams of my Father*, the author speaks warmly of an older black poet, he identifies simply as "Frank" as being a decisive influence in helping him to find his present identity as an African-American..."[97]

Accuracy in Media's Cliff Kincaid elaborates on this part of Obama's story. Frank Davis was, in fact, a known communist who belonged to a party subservient to the Soviet Union. The 1951 report of the Commission on Subversive Activities to the Legislature of the Territory of Hawaii identified him as a CPUSA member. What's more, anti-communist congressional committees, including the House Un-American Activities Committee (HUAC), accused Davis of involvement in several communist-front organizations.[98]

Davis' background, interests, and network of Chicago contacts would provide both information and access to groups with whom he sympathized, including the Weathermen and the SDS. At the time of this writing, it's not clear whether Davis suggested that Obama particularly connect with anyone when he went to Chicago. But it is clear that Davis appears to be the only link that led Obama to the Windy City.

THE COMPANY HE KEEPS

Barack Obama claims that he wants us to judge him by who he is, not by the statements or actions of others. Yet the best he can do to shape the discussion about his questionable relationships is to divert and obfuscate. It seems the presumptive Democratic nominee does not want us to get to know the *real* man, but to admire from a distance the flashy, smooth, style-over-substance public persona of the man who would be president. So the candidate's leftist associates, friends, and family better define the Obama behind the Elmer Gantry façade. Voters have a reason to fear Obama if they believe the old adage, "You are the company you keep."

The time has come for answers. The voters and the press have raised many questions surrounding Obama's close ties to nefarious organizations and a long list of politicians and other public figures whose agenda doesn't appear to be in sync with that of the country. For starters, it is *far past time* for Obama to come clean about his obvious close relationship with Bill Ayers and his friends. And, for example, it is imperative that we know what kind of organizations received grants while Obama served was on the boards of various Chicago foundations.

And these answers must come quickly—before Obama ascends to the presidency, before all three branches of the federal government march in lockstep, before he gains control of the FBI, the CIA, Homeland Security Department, and every other federal agency. Now is the time to demand answers, before we find ourselves living in Obama's America—which will be quite different from the America we have always known and loved.

For new, breaking information on Barack Obama since this book was published, please go to www.audacityofdeceit.com. If you have friends who would like to receive this chapter, or any of the chapters in this book, please refer them to the same Web site where they can download the chapter of their choice for free.

CHAPTER THIRTEEN

OBAMA'S SECOND-TERM RENOMINATION SPEECH

W*HEN AN IRISHMAN* like me writes a book, it's too much to expect I wouldn't engage in a little humor. All apologies to the ghosts of Oscar Wilde and Will Rogers.

I hope future generations will not consider this the re-incarnation of Nostradamus.

STATEMENT BY PRESIDENT OBAMA
Democratic National Convention, August 2012

As I accept your nomination for re-election as President of the United States, I want to list the changes that I have made and that you believed in:

- *Created the Second Amendment historical society—all are free to join.*

- *Passed a new immigration law to increase the number of Jewish refugees from the U.N. territory of Israel.*

- *Completed the integration of our military into the United Nations's peace keeping forces.*

- *Brought all American servicemen back to American shores.*

- *Legalized marijuana use for health and emotional purposes.*

- *Passed legislation giving equal rights protection to all Christian religions that are registered with the brand new Federal Department of Diversity.*

- *Passed legislation granting abortion rights to all women who wish to abort their children six months after birth.*

- *Issued an Executive Order banning: ANWR oil drilling; offshore oil drilling; coal mining in Pennsylvania and West Virginia; oil shale harvesting in Utah and Wyoming; and coal to liquid fuel production—all to conform with new clean air, water and land policies.*

- *Mandated the closing of America's 104 nuclear plants by the end of my second term.*

- *Passed legislation confirming you can buy a gun after passing a test, registering your gun, and agreeing not to use it.*

- *Appointed three excellent Supreme Court Justices: Hillary Clinton, Barney Frank, and Diane Feinstein.*

- *Awarded full voting rights to 90 percent of all felons on parole.*

- *Negotiated a loan with the Brazil, Russia, India and China to pay the 2013 American budget.*

- *Agreed to give Venezuela territorial rights to Puerto Rico for an improved energy contract.*

- *Re-opened trade with Mexico and Canada after a one year suspension.*

- *Established a national daily lottery for American medical patients on the waiting list for federally approved medical operations and procedures.*

- *Increased unemployment payments to $3,000 a month for twenty-four months.*

- *Passed the foreign real estate tax law giving tax relief to those foreigners buying second homes thus sparking a boom in real estate sales.*

- *Passed an immigration bill and a bi-lingual test to speed up the six-month wait for citizenship.*

- *Issued a carbon card to every citizen that must be presented under penalty of law when buying gasoline, riding an airplane or using electricity. Individual carbon rationing is now a reality.*

- *Congress has passed and I have signed the $5,000 yearly family deduction for all families that grow a sustainable vegetable garden on their property.*

I would also like to thank the thirty-eight states that passed an amendment to the Constitution removing the restriction on foreign-born citizens running for president. This puts an end to the vicious rumors that have plagued my presidency, and has opened up the way for the Republican/Liberal fusion ticket to nominate former Governor Arnold Schwarzenegger for president. He, of course, will face me in November.

We have come to an agreement between the Canadian Parliament and American congressional team working on the Canada-America merger to remove all Amendments to the Bill of Rights and replace them with Canada's version of government guaranties.

I strongly look forward to the coming merger with Canada which is a gentler, softer, and more liberal nation with less poverty, more equality, greater fairness and a level playing field. And today with

65 percent of Americans paying no taxes at all, we have less need for individual freedom, risky opportunity, hateful competition and disruptive dynamism.

Alright, so I attempted to inject a sense of humor into a political discussion. We know that most of these things can't happen—at least, not by the end of his first term.

—Brad O'Leary

For new, breaking information on Barack Obama since this book was published, please go to www.audacityofdeceit.com. If you have friends who would like to receive this chapter, or any of the chapters in this book, please refer them to the same Web site where they can download the chapter of their choice for free.

NOTES

Chapter One: Changing America's Social Values

1. Associated Press, "James Dobson Accuses Barack Obama of 'Distorting' Bible," *Boston Herald*, June 23, 2008.

2. R. Lizza, "Making It," *New Yorker*, July 21, 2008, available at http://www.newyorker.com/reporting/2008/07/21/080721fa_fact_lizza? printable=true.

3. D. Prager, "Why a Black Artist Replaced the National Anthem," *Townhall.com*, July 8, 2008, available at http://www.townhall.com/ columnists/DennisPrager/2008/07/08/why_a_black_artist_replaced_the_ national_anthem.

4. J. Whitesides, "Under fire, Obama clarifies small-town remarks," Reuters, April 12, 2008, available at http://www.reuters.com/article/ topNews/idUSN11166760200080412?feedType=RSS&feedName=topNews&rp c=22&sp=true.

5. C. Thomas, "Obama is No Joshua," *Townhall.com*, June 12, 2008, available at http://www.townhall.com/columnists/CalThomas/2008/06/12/ obama_is_no_joshua?page=1.

6. C. Thomas, "Obama is No Joshua," *Townhall.com*, June 12, 2008, available at http://www.townhall.com/columnists/CalThomas/2008/06/12/ obama_is_no_joshua?page=1.

7. D. Stokes, "Carter, Obama and the Evangelicals," *Townhall.com*, June 29, 2008, available at http://www.townhall.com/Columnists/DavidRStokes/ 2008/06/29/carter,_obama,_and_the_evangelicals?page=full&comments=true.

8. S. Kurtz, "Left in Church," *National Review Online*, May 20, 2008.

9. A. Bradley, "The Marxist Roots of Black Liberation Theology," Acton Institute, available at http://www.acton.org/commentary/443_marxist_roots_ of_black_liberation_theology.php?gclid=CPuB7NrEnZQCFQ4vHgod4jnAtg.

10. A Klein, "Christians copy Christ killers, says Obama's pastor's magazine," *WorldNetDaily*, May 20, 2008, available at http://www.wnd.com/ index.php?fa=PAGE.view&pageId=64828.

11. C. Falsani, "Obama: I Have a Deep Faith," *Chicago Sun Times*, April 5, 2004.

12. T. Harnden, "Barack Obama Denounced Priest for Mocking Hillary Clinton," *Telegraph*, May 30, 2008.

13. S. Kurtz, "Jeremiah Wright's 'Trumpet,'" *Weekly Standard*, May 19, 2008, Vol. 13, Issue 34.

14. R. Cherry, "Judeo-Christian Values," *American Thinker*, October 6, 2007, available at http://www.americanthinker.com/2007/10/ judeochristian_values.html.

15. Obama speech available at http://www.youtube.com/watch?v=tmC3IevZiik.

16. D. Brody, "Obama to CBN News: We're No Longer Just a Christian Nation," *CBN News*, July 30, 2007, available at http://www.cbn.com/ CBNnews/204016.aspx.

17. New Black Panther Party, "What the New Black Panthers Want; What the New Black Panthers Believe," available at http://www.newblackpanther.com/ 10pointplatform.html.

18. Transcript available at http://elections.foxnews.com/2008/04/28/ transcript-rev-wright-at-the-national-press-club/.

19. L. Farrakhan, Press Conference at Mosque Maryam in Chicago, December 22, 1999, available at http://www.finalcall.com/columns/mlf-press12-22-99.htm.

20. A. Klein, "National of Islam Activists on Obama Camp Payroll," *WorldNetDaily*, June 3, 2008, available at http://www.wnd.com/index.php? fa=PAGE.view&pageId=66167.

21. Source: FOX News/Opinion Dynamics Poll. July 15-16, 2003. N=900 registered voters nationwide. MoE ± 3.

22. B. Obama, *The Audacity of Hope*, pages 89-92, October 1, 2006.

23. M. Adams, "Fourth Letter to a Secular Nation," available at http://www.onenewsnow.com/Blog/Default.aspx?id=131086.

24. A. Mohler, "Is the Sanctity of Human Life an Outmoded Concept," The Albert Mohler Program, October 13, 2005, available at http://www.albertmohler.com/commentary_read.php?cdate=2005-10-13.

25. NARAL, "Pro-Choice America Fact Sheet on Barack Obama," page 1.

26. Supreme Court of the United States, GONZALES, ATTORNEY GENERAL v. CARHART ET AL., CERTIORARI TO THE UNITED STATES COURT OF APPEALS FOR THE EIGHTH CIRCUIT, No. 05–380. Argued November 8, 2006—Decided April 18, 2007, available at http://www.supremecourtus.gov/opinions/06pdf/05-380.pdf.

27. Pope Benedict XVI, "Address of His Holiness Benedict XVI to the Members of the European People's Party on the Occasion of the Study Days on Europe," March 30, 2006, available at http://www.vatican.va/holy_father/benedict_xvi/speeches/2006/march/documents/hf_ben-xvi_spe_20060330_eu-parliamentarians_en.html.

28. A. Carpenter, "Obama More Pro-Choice than NARAL," *Human Events*, December 26, 2006, available at http://www.humanevents.com/article.php?id=18647.

29. J. Stanek, "Pro-Life Pulse," available at http://www.jillstanek.com/bio.html.

30. J. Stanek, "Hearing on H.R. 4292, the "Born Alive Infant Protection Act of 2000."

31. J. Stanek, "Barack Obama and the Comfort Room," *WorldNetDaily*, June 18, 2008, available at http://www.wnd.com/index.php?fa=PAGE.view&pageId=67328.

32. Ibid.

33. Ibid.

34. B. Obama, "State of Illinois, 92nd General Assembly, Regular Session Senate Transcript," March 30, 2001, available at http://www.ilga.gov/senate/transcripts/strans92/ST033001.pdf.

35. Ibid.

36. J. Stanek, "When Obama Chose His Church Over His State," *WorldNetDaily.com*, July 10, 2008, available at http://www.wnd.com/index.php?pageId=39719.

37. Ibid.

38. Ibid.

39. Ibid.

40. Ibid.

41. B. Obama, "Education," available at http://www.barackobama.com/ssues/education/.

42. *Rolling Stone*, "Inside Barack Obama's iPod," June 25, 2008, available at http://www.rollingstone.com/rockdaily/index.php/2008/06/25/barack-obama-the-stevie-wonder-geek-returns-to-the-cover-of-rolling-stone/.

43. Jay-Z, "Is That Yo Bitch?" from the album *Vol. 3: Life and Times of S. Carter*.

Chapter Two: Changing the Second Amendment

1. Accessed at http://www.nrapvf.com/AtIssue/Default.aspx.

2. Independent Voters of Illinois/Independent Precinct Organization Illinois General Assembly Questionnaire—1996, under the heading "Finance."

3. Ibid.

4. Ibid.

5. Ibid.

6. Ibid.

7. Ibid.

8. C. B. Brown, "Obama aims for pro-gun vote," *Politico.com*, April 6, 2008.

9. Ibid.

10. "Barack Obama: Supporting the Rights and Traditions of Hunters," white paper posted on BarackObama.com campaign Web site, http://www.barackobama.com/issues/additional/Obama_._Western_Sports men.pdf.

11. C. B. Brown, "Obama aims for pro-gun vote," *Politico.com*, April 6, 2008.

12. Sen. Barack Obama in an interview with Radio Iowa, April 22, 2007, located online at http://learfield.typepad.com/radioiowa/2007/04/ clinton_edwards.html.

13. J. McCormick, "Obama: My Wife Sees Need For Rural Gun Ownership," *Baltimore Sun*, November 25, 2007.

14. Ibid.

15. J. Lott, Jr., "Obama and Guns: Two Different Views," Fox News, April 7, 2008, available at http://www.foxnews.com/story/0,2933,347690,00.html.

16. Ibid.

17. "ISRA Blasts Candidate Obama on His Record of Hostility Toward Law-Abiding Firearm Owners," statement by the Illinois State Rifle Association, August 24, 2004.

18. J. McCormick, "Obama: My Wife Sees Need For Rural Gun Ownership," *Baltimore Sun*, November 25, 2007.

19. Ibid.

20. K. Blackwell, "His Disturbing Pattern," *New York Sun*, February 21, 2008, available at http://www.nysun.com/opinion/his-disturbing-pattern/71591/.

21. J. Cook, Interview with *World Today*, October 1, 2003, transcript available at http://www.abc.net.au/worldtoday/content/2003/s957886.htm.

22. R. Peters, "A Gun Ban That's Half-Cocked Leaves Us All Potential Targets," *Sydney Morning Herald*, November 6, 2002.

23. 2008 Pre-Potomac Primary interview, *Politico.com*, February 11, 2008.

24. W. LaPierre, "An Individual Right Affirmed," *American Rifleman*, August 2008.

Chapter Three: Voting Rights Turned Upside Down

1. E. Feser, "Should Felons Vote?," *City Journal*, Spring 2005.

2. Pete Hegseth, "Why Obama Must go to Iraq," *Wall Street Journal*, June 5, 2008.

3. Available at http://www.youtube.com/watch?v=TDp8xYwIlfk.

4. J. Lott, Jr., "The Criminal Constituency," *Baltimore Sun*, February 16, 2006.

5. E. Feser, "Should Felons Vote?," *City Journal*, Spring 2005.

Chapter Four: War on Success

1. M. Barone, "Obama and Clinton Big Government Economic Plans Need Debate," *U.S. News and World Report,* April 11, 2008

2. I. Ayres and B. Nalebuff, "The Ticket to Savings," *Forbes*, May 22, 2006.

3. U.S. Department of Homeland Security, "Yearbook of Immigration Statistics: 2007," accessed online at http://www.dhs.gov/ximgtn/statistics/publications/LPR07.shtm.

4. "National Economic Accounts, Gross Domestic Product," *Bureau of Economic Analysis*, U.S. Department of Commerce.

5. Independent Voters of Illinois/Independent Precinct Organization Illinois General Assembly Questionnaire—1996, under the heading "Finance."

6. Linda Killian, "Will the Democrats Gain in Congress," *Boston Globe*, May 18, 2008. Also see Chris Cillizza, "Friday Line: How Many Seats will Democrats Gain in the Senate," *The Washington Post*, May 16, 2008, available at http://blog.washingtonpost.com/thefix/2008/05/friday_senate_line_5.html.

7. D. Mitchell, *"The Historical Lessons of Lower Tax Rates,"* The Heritage Foundation, July 19, 1996.

8. "The money squeeze: State's jobless rate now over 5%," *Seattle Post-Intelligencer*, June 17, 2008.

9. U.S. Department of Labor, "Unemployment rates in the European Union and selected member countries," June 6, 2008.

10. W. Beach, R. Hedermann, G. Nell, "Economic Effects of Increasing the Tax Rates on Capital Gains and Dividends," WebMemo #1891, The Heritage Foundation, accessed online at http://www.heritage.org/Research/Taxes/wm1891.cfm.

11. Ibid.

12. S. Forbes, "It's the Dollar, Stupid (and Taxes, Too)," *Forbes.com*, February 11, 2008.

13. B. Wilson, "Taxing Ourselves into Poverty," *Free Republic*, June 12, 2008.

14. White House Office of the Press Secretary, "Fact Sheet: Extending the President's Tax Relief: A Victory for American Taxpayers," May 17, 2006.

15. S. Hodge and B. Phillips, "Who Pays What on Tax Day," Tax Foundation, April 15, 2007.

16. Barack Obama, "Tax Fairness for the Middle Class," Obama '08 tax plan, found at http://obama.3cdn.net/b7be3b7cd08e587dca_v852mv8ja.pdf. Also see Scott A. Hodge & Brian Phillips, "Who Pays What on Tax Day," The Tax Foundation, April 15, 2007, found at http://www.taxfoundation.org/

research/show/22335.html (Note: 50 percent figure extrapolated from formula provided by Tax Foundation in this article).

17. S. Hodge and B. Phillips, "Who Pays What on Tax Day," Tax Foundation, April 15, 2007.

18. U.S. Department of Commerce, U.S. Census Bureau, *Income, Poverty and Health Insurance Coverage in the United States: 2006,* Table A-1. Households by Total Money Income, Race, and Hispanic Origin of Householder: 1967 to 2006, p. 29.

19. Ibid.

20. U.S. Department of Homeland Security, "Yearbook of Immigration Statistics: 2007," accessed online at http://www.dhs.gov/ximgtn/statistics/publications/LPR07.shtm.

21. National Center for Education Statistics, "College Enrollment and Enrollment Rates of Recent High School Completers, by Race/Ethnicity: 1960 through 2006," March 2008.

22. L. Mishel and J. Roy, "Rethinking High School Graduation Rates and Trends," Economic Policy Institute, April 2006.

23. U.S. Department of Labor, "College Enrollment and Work Activity of 2007 High School Graduates," April 25, 2008.

24. National Center for Education Statistics, "College Enrollment Rates of High School Graduates, by Sex: 1960 to 1998," August 1999.

25. Organisation for Economic Co-operation and Development, *Education at a Glance, 2005,* http://www.oecd.org/dataoecd/22/35/35282639.xls, Table A.1.2a, "Population that has attained at least uppersecondary education (2003)."

26. Gallup, "Americans Say Federal Income Taxes Too High, But Not Unfair," April 13, 2007.

27. Zogby International / ATI Values Poll, December 15-19, 2003 of 1,200 likely voters nationwide. Margin of error +/- 4.0 percentage points.

28. S. Moore, "Guess who really pays the taxes," *The American,* Nov./Dec. 2007 issue, accessed online at http://www.american.com/archive/2007/november-december-magazine-contents/guess-who-really-pays-the-taxes.

29. Ibid.

Chapter Five: Bankrupting America

1. C. Thomas, "CAN'T do spirit," *Insight* magazine, June 19, 2008.

2. The Internal Revenue Service, Table 6: "Internal Revenue Gross Collections, by Type of Tax, Fiscal Years 1960-2006 found at http://www.irs.gov/taxstats/article/0,,id=172265,00.html.

3. The National Taxpayers Union, "National Taxpayers Union Rates Congress," 1st Session, 2007., http://www.ntu.org/misc_items/rating/VS_2007.pdf; "National Taxpayers Union Rates Congress, 2nd Session, 2006, http://www.ntu.org/misc_items/rating/VS_2006.pdf.

4. Ibid.

5. Ibid.

6. The National Taxpayers Union, "Democratic Presidential Primary Spending Analysis—Barack Obama," 2008

7. "Barack Obama's Plan to Stimulate the Economy," available at http://my.barackobama.com/page/-/HQpress/011308%20Stimulus%20fact%20sheet.pdf.

8. "Barack Obama: Fighting Poverty and Creating a Bridge to the Middle Class," available at http://www.barackobama.com/issues/pdf/PovertyFactSheet.pdf.

9. Obama '08, "Economy," available at http://www.barackobama.com/issues/economy/.

10. Obama '08, "Barack Obama's Plan for a Healthy America," available at http://www.barackobama.com/issues/pdf/HealthCareFullPlan.pdf.

11. Obama '08, "Seniors and Social Security," available at http://www.barackobama.com/issues/seniors/.

12. Obama '08, "Barack Obama: Helping America's Seniors," available at http://www.barackobama.com/pdf/seniorsFactSheet.pdf.

13. Obama '08, "Economy," available at http://www.barackobama.com/issues/economy/.

14. Obama '08, Changing the Odds for Urban America," available at http://www.barackobama.com/pdf/UrbanPovertyOverview.pdf.

15. Obama '08, "Barack Obama's Plan for Lifetime Success Through Education," available at http://obama.3cdn.net/a8dfc36246b3dcc3cb_iem6bxpgh.pdf.

16. Ibid.

17. Obama '08, "Obama Outlines Plan to Strengthen America's Community Colleges at Northcentral Technical College," available at http://www.barackobama.com/2008/02/16/obama_outlines_plan_to_ strengt.php/.

18. Obama '08, "Economy," available at http://www.barackobama.com/ issues/economy/.

19. Obama '08, "Barack Obama's Plan for Lifetime Success Through Education," available at http://obama.3cdn.net/a8dfc36246b3dcc3cb_iem6bxpgh.pdf.

20. Obama '08, "Seniors and Social Security," available at http://www.barackobama.com/issues/seniors/.

21. Obama '08, "Barack Obama: Rebuilding the Gulf Coast and Preventing Future Catastrophes," available at http://my.barackobama.com/page/- /HQpress/020708%20Katrina%20Fact%20Sheet.pdf.

22. Obama '08, "Remarks of Senator Barack Obama to Chicago Council on Global Affairs," April 23, 2007, available at http://my.barackobama.com/ page/content/fpccga.

23. Obama '08, "Immigration," available at http://www.barackobama.com/ ssues/immigration/.

24. Obama '08, "Technology," available at http://www.barackobama.com/ issues/technology/.

25. C. Thomas, "CAN'T do spirit," *Insight* magazine, June 19, 2008

Chapter Six: Starving America

1. R. Collins, "Carter's Second Coming?" *Townhall.com*, June 13, 2008, available at http://www.townhall.com/columnists/RichardHCollins/ 2008/06/13/carters_second_coming.

2. Friends of the Earth Action, "National Environmental Group Endorses Barack Obama for President," May 3, 2008, available at http://action.foe.org/t/4027/pressRelease.jsp?press_release_KEY=367.

3. Ibid.

4. J. Goldberg, "ANWR Not the Frosty Paradise It's Cracked Up to Be," *Townhall.com*, June 13, 2008.

5. P. Knight, "Small Group of House Republicans Derails ANWR Drilling," *The National Center for Public Policy Research*, November 10, 2005, available at http://www.nationalcenter.org/TSR111005.html.

6. Arctic Power, "Worried About Fuel Prices? ANWR Equals 30 Years of Saudi Oil," April 1, 2001, available at http://www.anwr.org/Resources/ Worried-About-Fuel-Prices-ANWR-Equals-30-Years-of-Saudi-Oil.php.

7. Arctic Power, "Presidential Candidates Views on ANWR—The Democrats," available at http://www.anwr.org/archives/presidential_ candidates_views_on_anwr_a_the_democrats.php.

8. B. Lieberman, "Opening America's Waters to Energy Production: A Positive Step in the Fight Against High Energy Prices," *The Heritage Foundation*, June 19, 2008.

9. U.S. Department of Interior, "Outer Continental Shelf Oil and Gas Assessment 2006," available at http://www.mms.gov/revaldiv/ RedNatAssessment.htm.

10. Energy Tomorrow, "Offshore Production," available at http://www.energytomorrow.org/environment/Offshore_Production.aspx.

11. CNNMoney.com, "China, Cuba Reported in Gulf Oil Partnership," May 9, 2006, available http://money.cnn.com/2006/05/09/news/economy/ oil_cuba/index.htm.

12. Gallup, "Potential Actions to Reduce Today's High Gas Prices," May 28, 2008, available at http://www.gallup.com/poll/107542/ Majority-Americans-Support-Price-Controls-Gas.aspx.

13. L. Rohter, "Obama Camp Closely Linked With Ethanol," *New York Times*, June 23, 2008, available at http://www.nytimes.com/2008/06/23/us/ politics/23ethanol.html.

14. Ibid.

15. C. Alexander and C. Hurt, "Biofuels and Their Impact on Food Prices," September 2007, available at http://www.ces.purdue.edu/extmedia/ ID/ID-346-W.pdf.

16. B. Lieberman, "Ethanol and Other Biofuels: A Global Warming Solution Worse than the Problem," The Heritage Foundation, May 2, 2008, available at http://www.heritage.org/Research/Energyandenvironment/ wm1912.cfm#_ftn6.

17. Bureau of Labor and Statistics, "Consumer Price Index," available at http://data.bls.gov/cgi-bin/surveymost?ap.

18. E. Istook, "Ethanol: The Political Fuel," *The Heritage Foundation*, April 18, 2008, available at http://www.heritage.org/Press/Commentary/ed041808b.cfm.

19. *Los Angeles Times*, "Stop Requiring Ethanol Production," July 3, 2008, available at http://www.latimes.com/news/opinion/la-ed-ethanol3-2008jul03,0,2639886.story.

20. T. Patzek, D. Pimentel, M. Wang, C. Saricks, M. Wu, H. Shapouri and J. Duffield, "The Many Problems with Ethanol from Corn: ust How Unsustainable Is It?" available at www.phoenixprojectfoundation.us/user/The%20Many%20Problems%20of%20Ethanol.pdf.

21. *Los Angeles Times*, "Stop Requiring Ethanol Production," July 3, 2008, available at http://www.latimes.com/news/opinion/la-ed-ethanol3-2008jul03,0,2639886.story.

22.T. Searchinger, R. Heimlich, R. Houghton, F. Dong, A. Elobeid, J. Fabiosa, S. Tokgoz, D. Hayes, T. Yu, "Use of U.S. Croplands for Biofuels Increases Greenhouse Gases Through Emissions from Land-Use Change," *Science*, February 7, 2008, available at http://www.sciencemag.org/cgi/content/abstract/1151861.

23. Associated Press, "Corn Boom Could Expand 'Dead Zone' in Gulf," December 17, 2007, available at http://www.msnbc.msn.com/id/22301669/.

24 Los Angeles Times, "Stop Requiring Ethanol Production," July 3, 2008, available at http://www.latimes.com/news/opinion/la-ed-ethanol3-2008jul03,0,2639886.story.

25. S. Kroft, "France: Vive Les Nukes," *60 Minutes*, April 8, 2007, available at http://www.cbsnews.com/stories/2007/04/06/60minutes/main2655782.shtml.

26. D. Currie, "Power Surge," *The American*, January/February 2008, available at http://www.american.com/archive/2008/january-february-magazine-contents/power-surge.

27. P. Davidson, "How Risky is the New Era of Nuclear Power?" *USA Today*, December 12, 2007, available at http://www.usatoday.com/money/industries/energy/2007-12-11-nuclear-plant-safety_N.htm.

28. Reuters, "Obama Criticizes McCain's Nuclear Power Plan," June 24, 2008, available at http://www.reuters.com/article/politicsNews/idUSWBT00926320080624?feedType=RSS&feedName=politicsNews.

29. B. Obama, "New Energy for America," available at http://www.barackobama.com/issues/energy/.

30. Energy Information Administration, "U.S. Energy Consumption by Energy Source," April 2008, available at http://www.eia.doe.gov/cneaf/solar.renewables/page/trends/table1.html.

31. B. Obama, "New Energy for America," available at http://www.barackobama.com/issues/energy/.

32. Office of Management and Budget, "Department of Energy," available at http://www.whitehouse.gov/omb/budget/fy2005/energy.html.

33. F. Sissine, "Renewable Energy R&D Funding History: A Comparison with Funding for Nuclear Energy, Fossil Energy, and Energy Efficiency R&D," *Congressional Research Service*, April 9, 2008, http://fpc.state.gov/documents/organization/104708.pdf.

34. B. Obama, "New Energy for America," available at http://www.barackobama.com/issues/energy/.

35. American Coalition for Clean Coal Electricity, "Half Our Electricity Comes from Coal," 2008, available at http://www.americaspower.org/Issues-Policy/50.

36. American Coalition for Clean Coal Technology, "Factoids," 2008, available at http://www.americaspower.org/The-Facts/Factoids.

37. American Coalition for Clean Coal Technology, "Commitment," 2008, available at http://www.americaspower.org/Issues-Policy/Commitment.

38. A. MacGillis and S. Mufson, "Coal Fuels a Debate Over Obama," *Washington Post*, page A1, June 24, 2007, available at http://www.washingtonpost.com/wp-dyn/content/article/2007/06/23/AR2007062301424_3.html?nav=E8.

39. Ibid.

40. World Coal Institute, "Coal: Liquid Fuels," available at http://www.worldcoal.org/pages/content/index.asp?PageID=428.

41. M. Spring, "Could Coal Replace Oil," *MoneyWeek*, May 6, 2006, available at http://www.moneyweek.com/file/13377/could-coal-replace-oil.html.

42. S. Horsely, "Squeezing Oil Out of Stones in the Rocky Mountains," *National Public Radio*, May 23, 2006, available at http://www.npr.org/templates/story/story.php?storyId=5424033.

43. Project Vote Smart, "Amendment on Certain Energy-Related Programs, Including the Development of Oil Shale and Offshore Natural Gas," March 13, 2008, available at http://www.votesmart.org/issue_keyvote_detail.php?cs_id=17899&can_id=9490.

44. B. Obama, "New Energy for America," (no mention of "oil shale" as of June 27, 2008), available at http://www.barackobama.com/issues/energy/.

45. National Center for Health Statistics, "Deaths, Final Data for 2005," Table 27, available at http://www.cdc.gov/nchs/fastats/lifexpec.htm.

46. M. Stone, "Social Security: Safety Net in Need of Repair," *CPA Journal*, available at http://www.nysscpa.org/cpajournal/2005/805/perspectives/p12.htm.

47. Jimmy Carter, "The 'Crisis of Confidence' Speech," July 15, 1979, available at http://www.pbs.org/wgbh/amex/carter/filmmore/ps_crisis.html.

48. P. McIlheran, "Eating Too Much," *New York Sun*, May 23, 2008, available at http://www.nysun.com/opinion/eating-too-much/77398/.

49. D. Kreutzer, "Don't Fall for 'Windfall' Profits Tax," *The Heritage Foundation*, May 8, 2008, available at http://www.heritage.org/Press/Commentary/ed050808i.cfm.

50. D. Whitten, "Obama May Levy $15 Billion Tax on Oil Company Profit," *Bloomberg*, May 1, 2008, available at http://www.bloomberg.com/apps/news?pid=newsarchive&sid=aP_1wrIyt1Nc.

51. K. Marre, "Congressional GOP Leaders Hammer Obama on Gas," *The Hill*, June 11, 2008, available at http://thehill.com/leading-the-news/congressional-gop-leaders-hammer-obama-on-gas-2008-06-11.html.

52. U.S. Senate Roll Call Vote Number 223, Senate Amendment 1704 to H.R. 6, June 21, 2007, available at http://www.senate.gov/legislative/LIS/roll_call_lists/roll_call_vote_cfm.cfm?congress=110&session=1&vote=00223.

53. *Washington Times*, "Senate Votes to Raise Auto Mileage Standards," June 22, 2007, available at http://www.washingtontimes.com/news/2007/jun/22/senate-votes-to-raise32auto-mileage-standards/?page=1.

54. V. Klaus, "Blue Planet in Green Shackles," *Competitive Enterprise Institute*, 2007.

Chapter Seven: Free Trade, Free People

1. R. Reagan, "Radio Address to the Nation on the Canadian Elections and Free Trade," November 26, 1988.

2. R. Novak, "Big Labor's Trade Shutdown," *Washington Post*, June 19, 2008, p. A19.

3. K. Strassel, "Farewell New Democrats," *Wall Street Journal*, June 20, 2008, p. A11.

4. Ibid.

5. Ibid.

6. F. Harrop, "How Green Was NAFTA?," *Cagle Post*, April 8, 2008, http://www.caglepost.com/column/Froma+Harrop/6002/How+Green+Was+NAFTA.html.

7. A. From, "Confessions of a Pro-Trade Democrat," *Wall Street Journal*, June 9, 2008, Page A15.

8. J. Fund, "A Test for Democrats on Foreign Policy," *Huffington Post*, April 7, 2008.

9. Office of the United States Trade Representative, "Benefits of Trade to States," http://www.ustr.gov/Benefits_of_Trade/States/Section_Index.html.

10. Office of the United States Trade Representative, "Benefits of Trade," July 2006, http://www.ustr.gov/assets/Document_Library/Fact_Sheets/2006/asset_upload_file451_9646.pdf.

11. Ibid.

12. The Office of Trade and Industry Information (OTII), Manufacturing and Services, International Trade Administration, U.S. Department of Commerce, Table: "Exports Total", 1989-2007, http://tse.export.gov/MapFrameset.aspx?MapPage=NTDMapDisplay.aspx&UniqueURL=zqczm345o34phueg33dki3md-2008-6-29-16-35-22.

13. C. Broda & J. Romalis, "Inequality and Prices: Does China Benefit the Poor in America?," The University of Chicago, GSB & NBER, March 26, 2008, http://faculty.chicagogsb.edu/christian.broda/website/research/unrestricted/Broda_TradeInequality.pdf.

14. F. Zakaria, "What the World Is Hearing," *Newsweek*, March 10, 2008.

15. C. Farrell, "Two Cheers for Free Trade," *BusinessWeek*, March 27, 2008.

16. S. Graham-Felsen, "Obama's Economic Policy Address at Janesville GM Assembly Plant," Sam Graham-Felsen's Blog, Obama '08 Web site at http://my.barackobama.com/page/community/post/samgrahamfelsen/Cmzm.

17. R. Lowry, "The Global-Warming Bubble," *National Review*, June 20, 2008.

18. Dr. S. Wang, "China Needs Air Conditioning," *Forbes*, February 10, 2008.

19. S. Gottlieb, "The Democrats' Foreign-Policy Game," *Christian Science Monitor*, July 7, 2008, available at http://www.csmonitor.com/2008/0707/p09s02-coop.html.

Chapter Eight: Changing Justice

1. U.S. Department of Justice, Office of Legal Policy, "Judicial Nominations," available at http://www.usdoj.gov/olp/judicialnominations.htm.

2. B. Obama, "Obama to Vote No On Nomination of Judge Alito to the Supreme Court," U.S. Senate statement, released January 24, 2006.

3. Ibid.

4. E. Feulner, "Verdict's in on Alito," *Heritage Foundation*, November 9, 2005.

5. Ibid.

6. Ibid.

7. "American Bar Association Rates Alito 'Well-Qualified,'" *Voice of America*, January 4, 2006.

8. B. Obama, "Remarks of Sen. Barack Obama on the Confirmation of Judge John Roberts," statement issued by his U.S. Senate office, September 22, 2005.

9. Ibid.

10. T. Jeffreys, "Obama's Class-War Court," *Cybercast News Service*, February 27, 2008.

11. Ibid.

12. "California Ban on Same-Sex Marriage Struck Down," *CNN*, May 16, 2008.

13. N. Pickler, B. Fouhy, "Obama rebukes McCain camp on terrorism criticism," Associated Press, June 18, 2008.

14. Ibid.

15. "Al Qaeda, cohorts remain worst terrorism threat: U.S.," Reuters, April 30, 2008.

16. Editorial by *Wall Street Journal*, "Silver Bullet," June 27, 2008.

17. D. Savage, "Supreme Court blocs rarely wavered," *Los Angeles Times*, June 29, 2008, available at http://articles.latimes.com/2008/jun/29/nation.

18. Ibid.

19. M. Gryboski, "McCain, Obama differ on approach to judicial nominees," *Cybercast News Service*, June 16, 2008.

Chapter Nine: Changing American Healthcare

1. B. Dixon, "Barack Obama: Hypocrisy in Healthcare," *BlackAgendaReport.com*, January 31, 2007.

2. B. Obama, Speech in Iowa City, IA, May 29, 2007.

3. D. Morris, "The Debate McCain Must Force," *Real Clear Politics*, June 25, 2007, available at http://www.realclearpolitics.com/articles/2008/06/ obamas_new_strategy.html.

4. A. Carpenter, "Obama: Kids Should Learn Spanish," *Townhall.com*, July 9, 2008, available at http://www.townhall.com/Columnists/AmandaCarpenter/ 2008/07/09/obama_kids_should_learn_spanish.

5. Barack Obama for President Web site, Health Care, available at http://www.barackobama.com/issues/healthcare/ on May 19, 2008.

6. Ibid.

7. Ibid.

8. J. Goodman, PhD, "The Obama Health Plan," July 11, 2008, available at http://www.john-goodman-blog.com/the-obama-health-plan/.

9. Ibid.

10. R. E. Moffit., "The Cure: How Capitalism Can Save Health Care," *Lecture #982, Heritage Foundation*, Oct. 18, 2006.

11. Ibid.

12. Ibid.

13. D. Gratzer, M.D., "The Cure: How Capitalism Can Save Health Care," *Lecture #982, The Heritage Foundation*, October 18, 2006.

14. Ibid.

15. E. Tyrell, Jr., "Health Care from Adam Smith," *Human Events*, July 10, 2008, available at http://www.humanevents.com/article.php?id=27452.

16. Ibid.

17. M. Moore, "Social Security and Medicare Forecast 2005," *National Center for Policy Analysis*, Brief Analysis No. 510, April 7, 2005.

18. D. Gratzer, "For health care woes, a capitalism prescription," *Washington Post*, October 25, 2006.

19. Book summary, "Healthy Competition: What's Holding Back Health Care and How to Free It," by Michael F. Cannon and Michael Tanner, *Cato Institute*, accessed at http://www.catostore.org/index.asp?fa=ProductDetails&method=cats&scid=33&pid=1441272.

20. M. Tanner, "The Grass Is Not Always Greener: A Look at National Health Care Systems Around the World," Policy Analysis No. 613, *Cato Institute*, March 18, 2008.

21. Ibid.

22. Ibid.

23. S. Gottlieb, "Obama's Health Care Record," *Wall Street Journal*, May 6, 2008.

24. Ibid.

25. L. Rockwell, speech at Mises Circle in Seattle, Washington, "Everything you love you owe to capitalism," May 17, 2008.

Chapter Ten: Changing American Defense

1. G. W. Bush, speech before Israeli Knesset, May 15, 2008, transcript available at http://i.usatoday.net/news/mmemmottpdf/bush-knisset-may-15-2008.pdf.

2. USA Patriot Act summary, H.R. 3162 in the Senate of the United States, October 24, 2001.

3. K. Holmes, PhD, E. Meese III, "The Administration's Anti-Terrorism Package: Balancing Security and Liberty," The Heritage Foundation, Backgrounder #1484, October 3, 2001.

4. Ibid.

5. Ibid.

6. Ibid.

7. President George W. Bush, Discussing the USA Patriot Act before graduates of at the Ohio State Highway Patrol Academy, June 9, 2005.

8. Factcheck.org on 2008 ABC News/Facebook/WMUR-NH Democratic debate, January 5, 2008.

9. J. K. Wilson, "Barack Obama: The Improbable Quest," pp. 43-44, published Oct. 30, 2007.

10. Barack Obama, Democratic presidential candidate debate, Las Vegas, Nevada, November 15, 2007.

11. L. Flanders, The Contenders, p. 73, November 11, 2007.

12. L. Chavez, "Obama's tired old formula," Creators Syndicate, March 23, 2008.

13. Ibid.

14. G. Cucullu, "The Iraq Surge: Why It's Working," *New York Post*, March 20, 2007.

15. Ibid.

16. Ibid.

17. Ibid.

18. Gen. Petraeus "Drawdown in Iraq to Pre-Surge Levels Could Come Next Summer," Fox News, September 10, 2008.

19. P. Pillar, "Intelligence, Policy and the War in Iraq," Foreign Affairs, March/April 2006.

20. M. Barone, "Rethinking the Iraq critics," Creators Syndicate, May 12, 2008.

21. Ibid.

22. Ibid.

23. Ibid.

24. Z. Roth, "The U.S., Iraq and 100 Years," *Columbia Journalism Review*, April 1, 2008.

25. E. Labott, "Clinton, Obama in war of words over 'rogue leaders,'" CNN, July 25, 2008.

26. A. Koppel, J. King, "U.S.: North Korea admits nuke program," CNN, October 17, 2002.

27. "Anti-Israel threat is no Iranian joke," editorial, *San Francisco Chronicle*, October 31, 2005.

28. R. Wright, "Iranian Flow of Weapons Increasing, Officials Say," *Washington Post*, June 3, 2008.

29. Ibid.

30. 2007 Democratic debate at Saint Anselm College. June 3, 2007.

31. Congressional Black Caucus Democratic debate, January 21, 2008.

32. B. Obama, during an appearance on CNN's *Larry King Live*, March 19, 2007.

33. Senator Barack Obama, Congressional Record, 6/21/06, p. S6233.

34. E. Koch, "The Democrats' Plan to Demoralize Our Troops," *FrontPageMag.com*, May 17, 2007.

Chapter Twelve: Trust

1. B. Herbert, "Lurching with Abandon," *New York Times*, July 8, 2008.

2. Greg Sargent, "Obama Camp Says It: He'll Support Filibuster Of Any Bill Containing Telecom Immunity," Talking Points Memo's "Election Central" Blog, tpmelectioncentral.talkingpointsmemo.com, October 24, 2007.

3. McCormick, "Obama's Online Muscle Flexes Against Him," *Chicago Tribune*, July 8, 2008.

4. "Top Obama Flip-Flops," *Washington Post*, February 25, 2008.

5. "Obama's Flip-Flops," Associated Press, July 5, 2008.

6. Obama '08 Web site, "Sportsmen" at http://www.barackobama.com/issues/additional/#sportsmen.

7. United States Senate, S. 397, vote number 217, Kennedy amendment July 2, 2005.

8. Mike Allen, "Obama To Scrap Bush Faith-Based Office" *The Politico*, July 1, 2008.

9. "Obama to expand Bush's faith based programs," *Associated Press*, July 1, 2008.

10. Transcript: "Jake Tapper Interviews Barack Obama," ABC News, June 16, 2008.

11. Fox News, "Obama opposes California ballot measure seeking constitutional ban on same-sex marriage," July 1, 2008.

12. Political Bulletin: "Iran Tests Missiles Able to Reach Israel," *U.S. News & World Report*, July 10, 2008.

13. Editorial: "Mr. Zebari's Message, *Washington Post*, June 18, 2008.

14. Fox News Network's *Fox News Sunday*, April 27, 2008.

15. Hotair.com quoting ABC News, "ABC: Obama flip-flopped on welfare reform," July 1, 2008.

16. "Obama Flip-Flops on NAFTA," *World Net Daily*, February 26, 2008.

17. "Top Obama Flip-Flops," *Washington Post*, February 25, 2008.

18. Ibid.

19. Ibid.

20. Ibid.

21. Lynn Sweet, "Obama's Selma Speech. Text as delivered," *Chicago Sun-Times*, March 4, 2007.

22. According to the Obama campaign Website, Obama was born August 4, 1961.

23. University of Chicago press release, undated, at http://www.law.uchicago.edu/media/index.html.

24. Ben Wallace-Wells, "Destiny's Child," *Rolling Stone*, February 22, 2007.

25. Elias Crim and Matthew Vadum, "Barack Obama: A Radical Leftist's Journal from Community Organizing to Politics," Foundation Watch, June 2008.

26. Obama '08 Web site at http://my.barackobama.com/page/ community/group/MarxistsSocialistsCommunistsforObama.

27. NoQuarterUSA.net blog, "Ayers, Obama, Philanthropy, Corruption: What Big Media Refuses to Disclose about Obama's Checkered Past in Chicago Machine Politics, May 29, 2008.

28. Dinitia Smith, "No Regrets for a Love Of Explosives; In a Memoir of Sorts, a War Protester Talks of Life With the Weathermen," *New York Times*, September 11, 2001.

29. *New York Times*, "Transcript: Democratic Debate in Philadelphia," April 16, 2008.

30. Steve Diamond, "That Guy Who Lives in My Neighborhood: Behind the Ayers-Obama Relationship," Global Labor and the Global Economy blog, June 18, 2008.

31. Ibid.

32. Ibid.

33. Ibid.

34. Ibid.

35. University of Chicago press release dated Novemer 4, 1997, "Should a child ever be called a "super predator?," at http://www-news.uchicago.edu/releases/97/971104.juvenile.justice.shtml.

36. Conference Notice posted by the University of Illinois-Chicago, "Intellectuals: Who Needs Them?," April 2002 at http://www.uic.edu/classes/las/las400/conferencealt.htm.

37. Chris Fusco and Abdon M. Pallasch, "Who is Bill Ayers?," *Chicago Sun-Times*, April 18, 2008.

38. Political Wrinkles blog, "Mike Klonsky: Obama Blogger," June 25, 2008 at http://www.politicalwrinkles.com/elections/3723-mike-klonsky-obama-blogger.html.

39. Steve Diamond, "That Guy Who Lives in My Neighborhood: Behind the Ayers-Obama Relationship," Global Labor and the Global Economy blog, June 18, 2008 and updated June 23, 2008 to include the material on Mike Klonsky.

40. DiscoverTheNetworks.org, "Carl Davidson," at http://www.discoverthenetworks.org/individualProfile.asp?indid=2322

41. Lynn Sweet column, "Obama touts small donor network but also relies on high end "bundlers" for millions," *Chicago Sun-Times*, April 16, 2007.

42. Rezko Watch, "One-degree of separation: Obama's ultra-leftist backers—Part 1," April 28, 2008.

43. Rezko Watch, "One-degree of separation: Obama's ultra-leftist backers—Part 1," April 28, 2008.

44. Chris Fusco and Abdon M. Pallasch, "Who is Bill Ayers?," *Chicago Sun-Times,* April 18, 2008.

45. Rezko Watch, "One-degree of separation: Obama's ultra-leftist backers—Part 1," April 28, 2008.

46. Progressives for Obama blog at http://progressivesforobama.blogspot.com.

47. SpidelBlog, "Tom Hayden Endorses Obama," January 28, 2008.

48. DiscoverTheNetworks.org, "Tom Hayden," at http://www.discoverthenetworks.org/individualProfile.asp?indid=1334.

49. Ibid.

50. CNS News.com, "Dissecting Code Pink/Walter Reed Protesters," August 25, 2005.

51. John Perazzo, "Jodie Evans: Activist in Pink," *Front Page Magazine,* December 8, 2003.

52. Hot Air blog, "Jodie Evans: Code Pink Founder, Obama Bundler, Osama Apologist," June 12, 2008.

53. Dr. Lyle H. Rossiter, "The Liberal Mind: The Psychological Causes of Political Madness," *Townhall.com,* December 4, 2006.

54. Information found at Discover theNetworks at http://www.discoverthenetworks.org/funderprofile.asp?fndid=5340&category=79.

55. A. Klein, "Obama Worked with Terrorist," *WorldNetDaily.com,* February 24, 2008, available at http://www.worldnetdaily.com/index.php?pageId=57231.

56. Ibid.

57. Ibid.

58. P. Wallsten, "Allies of Palestinians See a Friend in Barack Obama," *Los Angeles Times,* April 10, 2008, available at http://www.latimes.com/news/politics/la-na-obamamideast10apr10,0,5826085.story.

59. Ibid.

60. Ibid.

61. "Obama's Northern Trust Connections," July 7, 2008 at http://therealbarackobama.wordpress.com/2008/07/07/obamas-northern-trust-connections/

62. Ibid.

63. Guy Benson, "Obama & Rezko: The Silent Scandal," *National Review Online Media Blog*, June 11, 2008

64. Ryan Lizza, "Making It: How Chicago Shaped Obama," *New Yorker*, July 21, 2008.

65. Chris Fusco and Tim Novak, "Rezko cash triple what Obama says," *Chicago Sun-Times*, June 18, 2007.

66. David Jackson, "Barack Obama: I trusted Rezko," *Chicago Tribune*, March 15, 2008.

67. Ibid.

68. Ibid.

69. Ibid.

70. Crim and Matthew Vadun, "Barack Obama: A Radical Leftist's Journal from Community Organizing to Politics, Foundation Watch, June 2008.

71. CBS 2 TV Chicago, "Obama Rejecting Criticism on Work with Tony Rezko," April 23, 2007.

72. Tim Novak, "Obama's letters for Rezko," *Chicago Sun-Times*, June 13, 2007.

73. Ibid.

74. Chris Fusco and Tim Novak, "Obama cuts Rezko ties," *Chicago Sun-Times*, January 30, 2008.

75. Aswini Anburajan, "Obama on his state senate records," MSNBC's First Read, November 9, 2007.

76. Ibid.

77. Ibid.

78. Ibid.

79. Ibid.

80. Judicial Watch press release, "Judicial Watch Files Senate, FEC Complaints against Barack Obama over Questionable Mortgage Loan," July 9, 2008.

81. Ibid.

82. Northern Trust Annual Reports at http://www.northerntrust.com/pws/jsp/display2.jsp?XML=pages/nt/0512/ 1134489876627_4.xml&TYPE=interior.

83. Lyle H. Rossiter Jr., M.D., "Mr. Obama and the Company He Keeps," undated material.

84. Tim Jones, "Barack Obama: Mother was not just a girl from Kansas," *Chicago Tribune,* March 27, 2007.

85. Ibid.

86. Jonathan Martin, "Obama's mother known here as 'uncommon,'" *Seattle Times,* April 8, 2008.

87. Barack Obama, *Dreams from My Father,* Three Rivers Press, 2004, p. 220.

88. Ibid., p. 278.

89. Barack Obama (Sr.), "African Socialism and Its Applicability to Planning in Kenya," July 1965.

90. Barack Obama, *Dreams from My Father,* Three Rivers Press, 2004, p. 100-101.

91. Laotze blogspot, "An American Expat in Southeast Asia," Jan. 23, 2007 at http://laotze.blogspot.com/2007/01/tracking-down-obama-in-indonesia-part-2.html.

92. *Kaltim Post,* January 27, 2007 at http://www.kaltimpost.web.id/ berita/index.asp?Berita=Utama&id=195481.

93. *Banjarmasin Post,* Jul. 9, 2006 at http://www.indomedia.com/ bpost/072006/9/depan/utama4.htm).

94. Dr. James Dobson, "Parents Fear Their Children's Teen Rebellion," Focus on the Family, June 10, 2007.

95. Barack Obama, *Dreams from My Father,* Three Rivers Press, 2004, pp. 75-76.

96. Ibid., pp. 96-98.

97. Ibid.

98. Cliff Kincaid, "Is Obama a Marxist Mole?" Accuracy in Media Report, March 18, 2008.

ABOUT THE AUTHOR

Brad O'Leary serves as resident of ATI-News, an online magazine and information Web site that provides links to more than 750 English newspapers and magazines worldwide.

O'Leary is also chairman of the Board of PM Direct Marketing, one of the country's leading Perception Management firms representing numerous U.S. senators, corporations and associations. He is also former president of the American Association of Political Consultants.

From 1993 to 1997, Brad O'Leary hosted a talk show program on NBC Westwood One that boasted two million listeners a day. He was also a cover story and feature writer for *USA Today Weekend Magazine* with 100 million weekly readers.

O'Leary is the author of eleven books, including:

— *Presidential Follies*

> *Human Events* called *Follies* "as one-sided and impertinent as all getout, and yet it's also acute, knowing and percipient, not to mention wonderfully readable."

> U.S. Senator Phil Gramm remarked: "Brad O'Leary is one of the most creative and experienced observers on the contemporary political scene."

> According to Bill Murchison of the *Dallas Morning News*, "Hallow and O'Leary entertain, educate and occasionally infuriate, all between the same set of covers."

— *Are You a Conservative or a Liberal?*

> According to *Roll Call*, "This...paperback is a fun test to show folks where they stand on the political spectrum."

> Rush Limbaugh said, "I took the test and [O'Leary] got it right."

— *Triangle of Death*

> *Publisher's Weekly* said *Triangle*, which is a compelling recount

of the fateful events that led to the death of President John F. Kennedy, put forth a "colorful theory, implicating a French heroin syndicate, the U.S. mob and the South Vietnamese government."

O'Leary is also the executive producer or producer of eleven television series and twenty-seven television specials, including these award-winning programs:

—*Ronald Reagan: An American President*

> *EGO Magazine* called it: "A gloriously comprehensive collection of the most memorable events in Reagan's life and presidency...a must have for any serious fan of the Gipper."

—*The Planet is Alive* (a documentary chronicling the life of Pope John Paul II)

> The *L.A. Herald Examiner* called it "pure magic."

> The *St. Louis Review* said it is "spellbinding."

> *Variety* calls it "extraordinary and compelling."